DOWNHILL
LIES
AND
OTHER
FALSEHOODS

DOWNHILL LIES AND OTHER FALSEHOODS

OR
HOW TO PLAY DIRTY GOLF

by Rex Lardner

Line drawings by Roy Schlemme

HAWTHORN/DUTTON
New York

Library of Congress Catalog Card Number: 72-7779.

ISBN: 0-8015-2198-X

17   18   19   20

CONTENTS

DOWNHILL
LIES
AND
OTHER
FALSEHOODS

1

Fore!

There are cynical souls who say the devil was abroad in the land on a long-ago day in the middle of the fifteenth century when some unknown genius, irked at the world and filled with hatred for his fellowman, invented the game of golf. He did not call it that; his name for it was *goff*. It sounds like an ejaculation of disgust, which is very appropriate to the game of golf. Ask any player.

I have often tried to put myself inside the head of this man who was out of his skull on that day when he made himself a little leather ball, filled it with feathers, and using a stick, tried to knock it into a hole in the ground. Fie, man! More curses have been heaped upon your head by succeeding generations of golfers than on

3

the heads of Hannibal, Napoleon, and Hitler all lumped together.

How Lucifer must have chuckled when that first leather ball plopped into its cup! The inventor could not have guessed what he was unleashing upon the world, but his satanic majesty knew! Because golf is a game that frays tempers, tempts a man to lie and cheat and steal and risk damnation and the scorn of his fellow players without the quiver of a muscle (until he is discovered falsifying his scorecard, that is).

Queen Elizabeth I played golf. It's a matter of record. But I'm willing to lay odds that the Virgin Queen ripped off a few resounding oaths before she finally tucked her clubs away and swore off this game that brings out the worst in so many of us.

Consider the poor golfer. He puts out hundreds, perhaps thousands, of dollars to buy the finest of equipment. He has clubs endorsed by the pro players, the greatest performers in the game, men who are into golf for the money it puts into their wallets, so you pay hard-earned dollars for their names scratched into the brightly shining surface of a driver, a nine-iron, or a putter. The bag must be of the very best leather obtainable, especially if you are a status player and intent upon keeping up your end with the Joneses. Your golf balls should be expensive, to give you the best "carry," which simply means that when you hit it, because of the terrific material that goes into it, it will go farther than the ball your opponent is using.

You will pay anywhere from $1,000 to $25,000 to join a private golf club. Either that or you stand on line for

hours at public links to wait your turn. I know players who rise at five in the morning, hurry out to a public course, sign their names to the register, go back to bed and sleep, and then show up at the course around eleven when their names are due to be called. All this for the purpose of whacking a ball into a hole.

Now consider. Wouldn't it be easier—and far cheaper —to merely pick the ball up and throw it at the hole? No clubs needed, no special clothes or equipment. You can dig a small hole in your backyard for such a purpose and avoid traffic snarls on your way to the course on Saturday and Sunday mornings.

It's crazy, man.

But golf is a form of lunacy, as I feel confident someone far more intelligent than I has already observed. It breeds confidence, but it also shatters illusions of grandeur. It has made grown men weep in despair. It has caused priests and ministers to utter naughty words, even to blaspheme—under their breaths, perhaps, but still. . . .

Now why all this furore about a mere game? I've never seen anybody playing dominoes or checkers get so emotionally involved in their game as to do these things. Except for a few behavioral ploys by Bobby Fischer, he and Boris Spassky conducted themselves like gentlemen at their chessboard. Oops! Pardon me. Bridge players are also affected with the same sort of golf lunacy, but that's material for a different book.

How is this game for wild men played?

The whole idea of golf is to hit a little white ball with very costly clubs of varying shapes and sizes to propel it into a hole sunk in a smooth stretch of carefully tended grass, called a green, in as few strokes as possible. Every swing at the ball is counted as a stroke. Even if you miss the ball completely, which golfers have been known to do upon more occasions than they will admit (even to themselves), it still counts as a stroke.

The ideal number of strokes properly required to play around a course is called par. Par is marked on your scoreboard, a little bit of printed pasteboard with the par for each hole marked opposite a blank space left for the individual player to insert his own score. This is the crux of the whole game—what goes in those empty spaces. But more about this later.

Naturally, you play this game on a game board, called a course. It has been named other things in the past five hundred years, but we'll stick to the proper nomenclature. The length of the course is determined by the amount of real estate in which one has to play around. Most courses consist of eighteen holes, though there are nine-hole courses, too. The length of these holes varies from about 150 yards of the toughest terrain you ever saw outside a military training camp to about 600 yards.

There are sand traps and bunkers, doglegs and hoglegs, which lie there waiting for you to dare their hazards. Otherwise pleasant men, very nice chaps all of them, known as golf-course architects, plan these courses. I've often thought how often they must chuckle to themselves as they ink out on blueprint paper an eighteen-hole golf course. I can hear their fiendish laughter now and mentally glimpse them as they roll around in convulsions on the floor after having toppled off their chairs in mirthful eruptions.

"Wait'll the poor bastards see this set of sand traps right in front of the green! I'll give them six inches in between to make it through them. Otherwise they'll have to chip over them and go beyond the green into the poison ivy and sumac I'll have planted at the edge of the woods."

He draws feverishly for a little while, then pauses.

Our imaginary golf-course architect has come up with a most brilliant idea. "I know what I'll do!" he exclaims triumphantly. "I'll put quicksand in a few of the sand traps. Our golfers will lose a lot of balls in those!"

He could be persuaded to forget the quicksand only when it was pointed out to him that a lot of golfers would get lost forever in those quicksand traps, too.

He protested, "Teach them a good lesson!"

However, since golf clubs make a lot of money from golfers, it was decided that quicksand in sand traps— though a basically marvelous idea—was not workable. Instead, why not do something more humane, like four doglegs with a lot of high trees at each angle of turn? With this kind of layout, good golfers will try to shoot over the trees to save a stroke and. . . .

Well, everybody knows how a tree can stop a golf ball.

More balls lost! More time spent hunting for the balls hiding in tangled shrubs and briar patches. To soothe

the architect, you let him make the briar patches especially thorny so they can stick into men's ankles and
snag women golfers' stockings.

Our architect is not satisfied. "It's too easy," he grum-
bles. He thinks a while, then his eyes light up. "I know
what I'll do! I'll build hills. Lots of hills so the player
is always shooting up one hill and down another. His
legs will ache; he'll feel like a drunken llama from walking on slopes all day long."

Anything to make it harder on the golfer.

The hills go in. Plenty of them.

Your chessboard and your bridge table are flat. Usually, they're very attractive, and masterpieces of the
furniture-makers' art. You sit down with admiration
for them in your eyes and reach for the chess pieces or
the cards with happiness glowing inside you. But your
golf course!

You stand on the first tee, and your eyes range out
over a lot of narrow fairways and wide roughs, tiny
lakes and big sand bunkers, hills and woods, and your
heart sinks. You know at once that your score is going
to have another ten strokes added to it (at least) before you wind up haggard and exhausted at the eighteenth hole and head for the friendly sanctuary of the
nineteenth.

The nineteenth hole, for you beginners, is the club
bar.

There you will down martinis and/or manhattans
and listen to other players curse the day they ever
heard of a driver or a putter. You will hear sob stories

that will touch your deepest sympathies, yet make you exult and glow inside yourself as Balboa must have exulted when he first saw the Pacific Ocean.

And for each story you hear, yours will not be so bad. You didn't take eight strokes on the fifth, nor did you lose three balls in the water hazard. You were out of the sand trap on the tenth hole that has won the nickname of the Heartbreaker in only one stroke.

Filled with martinis (or manhattans), your ears stuffed with such tales, you will conclude that you had a pretty good day, all things considered. Your confidence will swell, and you'll be eager to come back tomorrow or the next day and really teach this course a lesson.

Next day you return, filled with pep and pride, and you begin your play. Hah! Today you take ten on that dogleg fifth, you lose four balls in the lake, and you waste five strokes in the sand trap of the Heartbreaker alone. You swear at first, in exasperation. You blaspheme, along about the ninth hole, and by the fifteenth you are weeping bitter tears.

You spend three hours at the club bar, moaning over the fact that you can't quit the damn game because you've already paid your dues for the whole year. It could even be that your wife will have to come and get you, since you're absolutely unable to find your car, let alone drive.

You vow to her, after you take her tongue-lashing like a whipped cur, that you will never let golf get you down again. She is right—aren't wives always right—

it is only a game. It is really stupid for a grown man with the brains you have, successful in business and with a wonderful family, to become annoyed because a silly little ball just refuses to do what you want it to do.

You go to bed to sleep it off.

Golf is a game. Nothing more. You are convinced.

Then a funny thing happens on the way to work during the week. You meet other golfers, your friends and business acquaintances, and the talk gets around to slicing a drive or making a birdie, and the pulse quickens, the face flushes, the raw courage inside you begins to assert itself. Golfing lunacy is getting ready to strike again.

You think about your game on the way home.

This is bad.

Always, you convince yourself that you took your eye off the ball, you didn't keep your arm stiff on your shots, your stance was that of an old lady with crippling arthritis. Man, you can con yourself. You always do. You can't help it. No golfer ever born can avoid this malady which I term five o'clock tee fever.

This coming Saturday, you won't make those mistakes. Oh, no. Not *you!*

You know what you did wrong, now. You can lick that slice, cure that hook, avoid that blankety-blank sand trap. Of course you can. Any good golfer can, when he knows what he is doing wrong. And you do know what you were doing wrong, why you came in with that wretched score instead of the one you usually shoot. This is the result of five o'clock tee fever. It has hypnotic qualities; it causes you to lie to yourself and swear that those lies are the absolute truth.

You make up an excuse to slip away to the golf course and practice putts. Invariably, every putt drops, even to the twenty-footers. You are the conqueror of your golf game, master of yourself—until next Saturday when you get another chance to play.

This happens not once, not twice, but again and again. It is like a recurring illness, a form of mental malaria. All golfers are afflicted with it. It goes on for years or for as long as you play golf. It is unavoidable. True golfers know I speak the truth.

If any nongolfer is reading this, he is probably lifting his head and staring around him with wildly bulging eyes. Can such things be? he is asking himself. Are there really sensible human beings who do such things, just to put a little white ball into a hole in the ground?

The answer, sadly, is: Yes, there are. Millions of us. All afflicted by the same bug.

But in defense of us poor mortals, let me say that there is far more to golf than merely meets the eye. It is a constant challenge, not only with the course and the ball and your clubs, but also with yourself. Forget about your opponent, be he of the quality of Jack Nicklaus or Lee Trevino. It is you yourself who are your own worst enemy.

Still, there is hope.

For us who are not the greatest golfers in the world, for us duffers who rarely break one hundred (golf slang for the fact that it takes you at least one hundred strokes to accomplish what your good pro player will do in sixty-eight or seventy), I hold out a helping hand. I have suffered from five o'clock tee fever, I have shanked balls, my normal game is a hook and slice on rye grass, I've toyed with the idea of buying up roughs and replacing them with foam rubber to help the bounce of my ball as it wends its merry way from tree trunk to tree trunk. I well know how you feel, at times.

But I have done something more than this, I like to think. Since golf is such a personal game, your own individual psyche is involved in every drive, every putt. Few people pay attention to this. Not only have I paid attention, I have made it my golf game. Quite literally. These days I psych myself—and my opponents—around courses, and win.

It may even work for you.

2

Putter-ing Around

You play the game with golf clubs. Yeah, yeah, I know you know this, but you just haven't stopped to think about the ramifications of this statement. Do you know that golf clubs are designated A, B, C, D, and E because of their swing weight? E is the heaviest club type, A the lightest.

The next thing to consider is shaft flexibility. Some players like a stiff shaft; others prefer one that whips around and into the ball. These club shafts are typed as X, S, R, A, and L.

There are four woods: the driver, the two-wood, which used to be known as the brassie, and the two spoons, designated as three-wood 'and four-wood, which differ mainly in the loft that the sloping face gives your ball. Some players will substitute a five-wood (with still more loft to the club face) for the two or three. The driver is used off the tees, for carries of roughly 200 to 265 yards, though a pro like Lawson Little or some of the other heavier belters might do upward of 300 yards off the tee. The brassie and three-wood are employed for a second long shot, ranging from 180 to 250 yards, depending on the caliber of individual play. The other two clubs have lesser lengths in their carries.

There are nine irons, a pitching wedge, a sand wedge, and a putter. Some golfers carry more than one putter. The two-iron, which used to be known as the cleek, is for shots needing about 185 yards distance. The seven-iron and eight-iron are for carries of 125 to 145 yards or thereabouts.

I mention all these clubs because you can accomplish wonders with them when playing with your opponents. Your main attack is his clubs. You question his use of one or the other, when it seems appropriate, and you put worry lines on his face by intimating that he chose the wrong club, that he would do better with a different one. You take his mind off the shot, see? He just has to ask himself, "Is my good friend right? Maybe I would get more carry with a number three."

You have accomplished your goal in a perfectly legal way. You've made him begin to worry. After a time he may look at you surreptitiously, just by moving his eyes and raising his eyebrows. You nod your head solemnly or give it a little sideways shake. Nothing too obvious, now. You're acting the role of friend and coun-

selor—you don't want him to think you're trying to talk him off his game. Which you are, naturally, but he mustn't think so.

When he makes a good shot with the wrong club, as sometimes happens, you do not gnash your teeth or stamp your foot. You rush up to him and cover him with congratulations. He will continue asking you for advice, and you will very gladly give it to him. Because he *won't* go on making good shots with the wrong clubs, and then he'll begin to worry about something else, like his stance.

Shafts of the woods are longer than those of the irons. Therefore, advise him to stand closer to the ball while driving and farther away when using an iron. This will sometimes make him miss the ball completely. This counts as a stroke, incidentally, and is known in golfers' jargon as a whiff.

You can also worry him by going back to swing weight and talking about it knowledgeably. Bone up on this with your golf pro first, or read a good text on golf. At the very worst, act as if you know what you're talking about when you observe gently, "Jim, I think your swing weight is all wrong for a big, strapping guy like you."

If he's anything like my friends, he'll wrinkle his brows and ask helplessly, "Swing weight? What in hell is swing weight? You mean I got to worry about another facet of this blankety-blank game?"

You have him in the hollow of your hand at that point. Don't push at a time like this. Say something like, "Jim, forget it. Sorry I brought it up."

He'll be on his knees to you, begging you to enlighten him about swing weight. You will then tell him, quite learnedly, that the weight of his club in proportion to his strength and the gusto of his swing play a very definite part in the manner in which he plays golf. You also explain that the flexibility of his shaft may be his problem and then point out that instead of an S, he may need an X.

He may or may not run gibbering to the golf pro. But you've won this particular round, at any rate. He won't be worth a nicked Spalding after that.

Another good way to disturb your opponent is to put your hand on his shoulder as you march along the fairway and say in confiding tones, "Jim, what you really should be using in that sand trap up ahead is a track iron."

This is guaranteed to bring him to a dead halt, always providing he isn't about a hundred and one years old and can remember the horse-and-buggy days.

"I never even heard of a track iron," he'll protest, turning pale.

He carries twenty clubs in his bag, but not a track iron, that's for sure. A track iron was used in those long-ago times back before the turn of the century to sock a ball out of a rut caused by horse-drawn maintenance wagons. It's really nothing more or less than a sand wedge, anyhow, but he doesn't know this. He'll be thinking about a track iron for the rest of the eighteen holes. His game will suffer, believe me.

Maybe even the golf pro will never have heard of a track iron. Think of how smart you'll seem to your opponents when you mention such things with that knowing look. If you also throw in a word or two about a gooseneck niblick, they'll think you're a goddam genius.

You see what you can do with just a smattering of wisdom about golf clubs. Already, you're a master psychiatrist. In the old days clubs had hickory shafts. Throw in a comment or two about how much better they were than the modern ones, or even vice versa. Anything to convince the opposition that you know what you're talking about. Next time you offer advice, they'll listen, all right.

If you're lucky enough to have a father, mother, or even an Aunt Minnie who might have an old set of golf clubs hanging around the attic or the cellar, try to lay hands on them. One particular club to borrow or even buy from Minnie is the putter. Putters are the secret weapons of golf. I have seen grown men weep in frustration because their putting couldn't match their wood or iron play.

Imagine it. You have taken four to get on the green. Your opponent has taken only three. You putt out in one. He takes three or maybe even four putts. This is a hole you have won, man. You've really won it big if you've used Aunt Minnie's old gooseneck, telling your disgruntled opponent that those old wooden putters with the iron facing have it all over the modern ones.

He'll worry about that damn putter all the way through five martinis. It gives you a psychological edge. Never, never, let him use it. He might discover it doesn't work any better for him than his own fifty-dollar job.

It helps to be a good putter when you use this ploy. It also helps if your fellow player is a lousy golfer. In my opinion putting in golf is like forward passing in football. It can save you a lot of tough yardage.

Anyone physically able to hit a ball can drive and use an iron. So it takes you an extra stroke or two to reach the green. If you are a good putter, you can often make this up by sinking putts of fifteen or twenty feet. And the psychological edge you get when you drop a twenty-footer is like Joe Namath unloading the bomb. You wear down your opposition, hole after hole.

One note to memorize in putting: Always keep your eye on the ball and even on its original position after your putter has made contact and the ball is rolling merrily toward the cup—hopefully—to drop in with that sweet little clunk that tells the whole world you have just putted out in one.

If Aunt Minnie has a seven- or eight-iron, and you do some secret practicing with it until you become reasonably good at it, it might help win your golf games, too. Nothing is so devastating to an opponent as to see you drag out a beat-up old club and perform miracles with it. It shatters his morale instantly. And this is the whole idea behind your psychological game.

The same thing applies to any other iron, such as the old-fashioned cleek (the two-iron) or the driver. Some of these old clubs may be warped. The shafts were made of wood in those days. If you can still use it with reasonable success, claiming that the warp helps you in some mysterious fashion, a good gambit to use is to say, "This crooked shaft helped cure my slice,

Jim!" In no time at all you'll have him biting his nails down to the quick.

You can also point out that sometimes a physical defect can be turned into a handicap. Mention Three Fingers Brown, the old-time Chicago Cubs pitcher, or Jim Dempsey, of more recent date, who with half a right foot still kicks tremendous field goals.

This will really get your opponent down. He has no one to turn to for help against such a weapon. He has no Aunt Minnie, no golf clubs that look as if they'd been through a mangler. There is nothing he can do. You have it made, because you possess a weapon he can't possibly lay hands on.

I grant you, this is an exceptional case, but there are other ways of combating the very excellent golf of your fellow players. The clubs themselves are merely a beginning. I'll talk about other methods later on.

While we're on golf clubs, I want to bring to your attention the trick-shot artists of this game. Some of them are very well known; they have given performances for awed onlookers, in which they can make the ball do everything but talk, all because they have made themselves masters of the clubs they use to perform these trick shots.

Two very well known trick-shot artists are Joe Kirkwood and Paul Hahn. I have stared in utter fascination as these experts make a ball jump over another and roll into the cup on the green, or put such spin on a ball that it will hit the ground and roll back to them as though it were a boomerang.

How do they do it? First of all, they have mastered the stroke; they know just how to use the club to hit the ball at the precise angle that will cause it to perform those prodigies of motion that make the audience gasp. A little click of clubhead meeting ball and the round white thing that gives most players heartaches and headaches jumps into the air or rolls in a circle or does just about anything you can name.

The reason I mention these trick-shot artists and call them to your attention is this: You can add them to your mental bag of golf psychology.

Who among us has not lofted a ball high into the air from the tee and only about fifty feet out? It is a flub, a badly hit ball. It is a disgrace to the name of golf.

Ah! But need it be?

Assuming you have made such a blunder, you do not curse or scowl or kick your inoffensive caddy. No, anything but. You turn to your fellow player and say, "It took me a long time to learn that trick."

Of course, he will think you have rocks in your skull.

You follow up your original statement with, "Every once in a while, when I'm not being pressed, I like to wing off one of those."

You see what you are doing? First of all, you're telling your opponent in a nice way that he isn't putting much pressure on you and that you fully expect to beat him. Naturally, this will make him fret. He'll begin thinking, "Jeez, this guy has ice water in his veins, to waste a stroke like that just for the sheer fun of it!"

He will begin making mistakes, believe me. You'll be able to catch up to him in your stroke count even before you get to the green.

You must practice on this one, however. It's almost instinctive to utter an epithet when you have blundered so badly. Muscular control of the face at such a time is all-important. Force yourself to smile. Get that smile into your eyes and into your voice, too. Don't just paste a silly grin on your face while your eyes depict the agony that is churning inside you.

If you're really a good liar, you may offhandedly say as you walk to play your second shot about a foot from the tee, "Learned that one from Joe Kirkwood." This is bound to impress.

The same technique is usable after you've made a spectacular shot. When I was a young man, I actually hit one of those rare shots when everything goes even better than you'd hoped. It was an uphill shot with the green just beyond the crown. My ball soared high up the hill and over the crown, to roll to a dead stop a foot from the hole.

I've never hit one like that since. But being young, I was swollen with pride and importance as I trudged up the hill and saw the golf pro standing there, a dour Scotsman with a briar pipe between his lips, who had been an interested spectator.

"Not bad, was it?" I asked, floating on air.

He took the pipe from his mouth. "Aye," he nodded, eyes twinkling, "everybody can't help but hit one right, once in a while."

I was utterly deflated.

So I speak out of bitter experience when I tell you that every so often you are going to hit a miracle shot, one of those that awe the onlooker and make you think —by God, you really can play this game! This is the proper moment to mention, as your fellow player congratulates you (hopefully), that you learned that one from Arnie Palmer. Or Lee Trevino. Or Jack Nicklaus. The name isn't too important, so long as it's one of the greats.

"Watched him on the fifth at Merion," you add.

It makes you out to be a real buff, a knowledgeable sort of guy. Maybe you did see him on the fifth at Merion, on television or in real life, but that's unimportant. The main thing is, let your opponent get the feeling that by merely watching a pro, you can adapt your style to his. It gives the other man the shakes.

I suppose I'd better mention the grip here, which means simply how you hold your club. A lot of the experts use the interlocking grip, in which you lay the handle across your left palm, fold the thumb over it, and then place your right hand so the palm lies against the shaft below your left hand. Close the fingers of your right hand about the shaft and then interlock the pinkie of the right hand between the index finger and forefinger of the left. This gives you control of the club. Jack Nicklaus uses this sort of grip. So does Gene Sarazen.

A second grip—one preferred by most pros—is the overlapping grip, first popularized by Harry Vardon. The club is placed pretty much the same way in the left hand with the left thumb and forefinger forming a

"V." The right hand closes over the shaft with the thumb and first three fingers positioned close to the left while the pinkie overlaps or rests on top of the left forefinger.

Some players prefer the baseball hold, in which you hang onto the golf club as you would a baseball bat, but I have never been able to do this because I don't feel that I have the proper control of the club.

The stance comes next. This is the position your body takes when you are about to hit the ball. There is the square stance, with the feet apart and set firmly on the ground, the toes touching an imaginary line that should point in the direction in which you want the ball to travel.

The open stance is one in which your left foot is drawn back slightly from this imaginary line. You adapt this stance when you want the ball to slice, or travel from left to right.

A third position, the closed stance, has the right foot drawn back from the imaginary line of flight and is used to combat the tendency of right-handed players to slice.

Now you begin your swing. As a right-handed player, you should try to pull the club through the shot with your left hand and arm without getting too much right hand into the shot. The right hand, of course, provides some of the power, but it also acts as a guide. Keep your left arm stiff as you cock your club above your shoulders, keep your eye on the ball, make your swing, hit the ball, and follow through.

Sounds easy, right?

But the greatest players in the world will sometimes inadvertently not do all of these things. Now, the pros practice endlessly until their grip, their stance and address, and their swing become almost completely automatic. Ben Hogan is a fine example of this. He taught himself to perfect his golf game by iron will and determination. It took him years, but at one time, back in the forties and the fifties, even other professionals stood in awe of him.

When Ben Hogan was so critically hurt in the auto accident that nearly killed him, he came back to golf almost crippled. Yet so well had he taught himself the right strokes and the proper address and follow-through that his body responded to his will, and in less than a year he was out on the circuit again, winning tournaments.

It can be done. You need time to practice and the iron determination to turn yourself into a good golfer. Most of us are only mere human beings, however, so I say, do the best you can.

But bone up on your psychology.

Never try to whack the bejesus out of the ball with your driver, fairway woods, or irons. Some men—Jack Nicklaus is one—can hit a drive for more than 300 yards. Be content with lesser distance and more accuracy.

Stay on the fairway if you can. Sacrifice distance to this goal. Me, I'm playing in the rough half the time. I never could follow my own advice. Just meet the ball.

Your swing will prove more powerful than you think. And the golf ball is a lively ball, like the one they use in baseball.

Men like Hank Aaron who hit a lot of home runs rarely try to hit them. They go up to the plate with the idea of meeting the ball. If they meet it squarely, it will carry for a long distance, even as your golf ball will when you stroke it properly.

You swing with your body and hit with your hands, is an old adage. All this means is that your backswing must be executed with your feet in the proper stance, your weight shifting to the right foot, the body bending and pivoting at the hips, after which comes the smooth flow of the downswing, the shift of weight to the left foot. Just when the clubhead is about to meet the ball, your hands take over in a completely instinctive action. They direct the club, the angle of the stroke. When you use your hands correctly in this regard, you're well on your way to perfecting your entire game.

In the follow-through your right heel, if you are a right-handed person, loses contact with the ground, the foot bending. Look at any picture of a golf pro as he completes his follow-through. Ask yourself if you do this, if you look like that when you finish your stroke. Have your wife or girlfriend take snapshots of you at various times in your stroke. You might be able to learn something from these pictures.

The clubs and their use are most important. You are always using a wood, an iron, or a putter when you play golf. And there are varying rules for their use. If you intend seriously to play this game, my advice is to see a pro and take some lessons.

You have to be able to play a reasonably good game, after all, for your psychological gambits to have any merit. No duffer who shoots a course in 140 or 150 can possibly hope to defeat a player who can go around in 80 or 85 unless he is spotted about two strokes a hole or more, and there's no way anybody will ever do that. Especially if they're playing for cold, hard cash.

Most players experience the greatest difficulty with their iron shots. For some reason, everyone can swing a driver and connect with the ball, possibly because it's elevated off the ground on a tee. And in one way or another, even a duffer can putt a ball. Ah, but those irons!

I have often thought that the old terms were the best. A cleek, a mashie, a niblick, a mashie niblick. Those names lent a bit of substance to a golf club. When you were on the fairway and needed a fairly long ball, you grabbed a club we now call the two-iron. Today's player would have the option of using a five-wood. If you needed a pitch onto the green, you knew that a mashie niblick was necessary. Today, that would be a six-iron, though most contemporary golfers lean toward using a seven-iron in that situation.

The irons range from one to nine, plus the pitching wedge, also called a ten-iron (though the average player seldom carries a one-iron, so that most sets range from the two-iron to the pitching wedge). My mind boggles when I consider the ramifications of each number. Oh, you get used to it in time, but if you're thinking about your daughter's birthday and she's just turned nine and you say "nine" unthinkingly, your caddy will hand you a nine-iron and there you'll be, pitching for a short distance when you ought to be socking away for a 150-yarder.

They harm your game, such slip-ups.

I don't suppose there's much we can do about the numbered irons, though. Everybody else seems satisfied with them, so we'll just have to go along and learn to use them. One thing to remember is that the irons have a shorter shaft than do the woods, which means simply that you have to stand closer to the ball when using them.

This is not an insurmountable obstacle. I know some players who use a three- or four-wood, depending on the loft of the club's face, when most players would go for a two- or three-iron. For some reason, the feel of the spoon gives those people more confidence. And golf is a game of confidence; otherwise there would be no purpose in attacking an opponent with psychological warfare.

Still, the two- or three-iron is the club to use when you have that fairway lie with about 150 yards needed to carry you to the green. The ball rests there, taunting you, on its padding of green grass. It seems like such an inoffensive thing. But you know the deviltry that lies in its hard little heart. Unless treated properly, it will do more tricks than somebody like Joe Kirkwood ever thought of. You want to reach the edge of the green, or even the green itself.

You address the ball. You stand closer than you do

for your drive or fairway wood shot. You draw back your arms, keeping the left arm straight, your eyes on the ball. Somewhere in the back of your head is the injunction that you hit your irons *down*.

This means that you hit under the ball, rather than against it, as you do with the driver and brassie. The idea here is that by hitting down at the ball, you lift it up. Sounds crazy, I know, but it's the truth.

Keep your feet slightly more parted on a long iron shot than on the pitch. On the long iron the ball would be in the middle of your stance or just a shade right of center toward your right foot. On the pitch your feet are closer together, the ball on a line with your right heel.

You swing downward. Your clubhead comes under the ball, and as your wrists uncock, they furnish you with the power to lift the ball up and away. You reach 150 yards. Just shy of the lip of the green, but a dog-gone good iron shot.

This game isn't as difficult as it seems, right? Wrong! All wrong! Wait'll the next time you try that two- or three-iron. You'll hook it, slice it, drive it off the fairway. If you're anything like me, that is. But maybe you're a good player and unafflicted with normal human failures.

Theoretically, every iron shot should be the same as the last one, always assuming you have followed your golf pro's advice. It's like making coffee, which is really nothing more than an experiment in which, if you use the same kind and amount of coffee, the same amount of water, and the same degree of heat every time, your cup of coffee should always be the same. Unfortunately, it is not, as we all know. But it should be—that's the point. It's the same with your golf shots. If you do the same thing again and again, all your two- or three-iron shots ought to be 150-yarders or better, and straight as an arrow. I know, I know, they're not. Neither are mine.

So you become a philosopher. You accept the fact that you're a human being and that a human being is prone to errors. Why curse and swear about it? You *know* you're going to goof on a good number of shots before you tee up your first ball. Accept the fact. I mean, really *accept* it. Even joke about it if it helps you. While you're playing your psychological game against your opponent, you must never show dismay at any of your flubs. This will shake the other guy's confidence. If you can grin after slicing a shot off the fairway, chuckle and say, "It's about time for that bad shot!" You'll be surprised at the effect on your fellow player.

He'll begin by staring at you goggle-eyed. Your lousy game doesn't disturb you—you even expect it. This goes against all the rules of golf, which means that your opponent will think you're some sort of superbeing, not human at all. It will affect his game, this marvelous attitude of yours. If he's the high-strung type, he may even go to pieces after a while. All because you laugh at your mistakes, you never get mad at yourself, you never curse the fates or break a golf club.

He knows such conduct isn't human. It annoys him in some way he doesn't understand, and after a time his own play will be adversely affected. Maybe he's even counting on your getting mad. When you don't, it throws him off-balance. Let him be the one to lose his temper.

He can't get mad at you, because you're all smiles and good nature. You admit you're going to play bad shots every so often. Why, he may even get a faint glimpse of a golden halo over your head around the sixteenth hole. I've never known this to happen, quite truthfully, but it *could.* I mean, after all, such conduct in the face of bad shot after bad shot may turn you into a real saint. Or win you a purple heart. Who knows?

Anyhow, the other guy will keep thinking about you and your eternal good nature, your happy acceptance of bad shots that would have him jumping into the water hazard, so that his game will begin to disintegrate. Add this to your golfing grab bag of psycho tricks.

Okay, then. You've made one of your few really good shots of the day, and you're close to the green. You grab your pitching wedge or your eight- or nine-iron, and you address the ball as I've mentioned. The big idea here is just to meet the ball. You want to lift it over the ridge and onto the green. You don't want it to roll across the green and down the other side, as so many of mine are prone to do.

Concentrate on just meeting the ball. Not hard, now. Easy does it. You hit downward, under the ball, and loft it in a smooth arc. Your ball hits the green and rolls. Maybe the gods will smile at you, and the ball will hit the stick and drop into the cup.

However, few of us are actually skilled enough to sink

a ball from a pitch-shot position. An Arnold Palmer or Gary Player perhaps, but not such as you or I, except when Lady Luck is hitting us with her magic wand.

Say you wind up six inches from the cup.

This is a beautiful lie. It may do one of two things: Either it will spur your partner to do his best to sink a thirty-footer or it will worry him so much he'll take three putts to hole out. The second consideration need not trouble you; it's the first one you must forestall.

So you make him relax, subconsciously.

Instead of jumping up and down with joy; you make a face and say, "Boy, I hate those short putts. I always tighten up on them."

This will make your opponent relax a little. He'll figure you will take two strokes to sink the ball, and he won't try that thirty-footer in a do-or-die attempt for victory. He will merely try to nudge the ball close to the hole rather than try to sink it.

Now it is your turn. You fret and worry vocally, but you sink the putt. You have outwitted him, but you don't let him know it. You turn a beaming face toward him and say, "Man, that won't happen again in a month of Sundays."

This will make him think that maybe you're just lucky today. Now he has not only you to beat, but your luck. It adds to his problem, and that's what you're always trying to do in this psychological game—pile woe and worry on your fellow player.

Naturally, having won this hole, the honor is yours of driving off first on the next tee.

You begin all over again.

Always remember: You must hit the ball. By this I mean you mustn't try to push it or scoop it up. And don't try to hammer it too long and too far. At the expense of accuracy, that is. It's better to have your tee shot land on the fairway and fifty yards short than have it go screaming off into the rough or be lost forever in a patch of woods.

Play straight down the fairway (if you can).

Let the other guys go for the distance records.

Control yourself first, then you can always control your clubs.

3

It's All a Matter of Course

As I have already noted, you play this game of golf on a board that consists of a lot of real estate. The technical name for your board is "course."

And therein lies the fun—because a golf course can be easy, it can be difficult, and it can be just about impossible. Most courses will have a couple of short holes, where the par is three. One of these is usually a water hole, meaning that between the tee and the green is a lovely little expanse of water just waiting to drown your ball.

Usually there will be a dogleg or two, meaning that you cannot see the green from the tee because it's hidden by trees. You will have to shoot down the fairway, then when you arrive at the angle of the dogleg, you see a lot more fairway and at the end of that, a little red or white flag flapping that shows you where the green is.

Some great players will shoot over these trees.

Don't you dare!

Just keep playing your regular game. Leave the fancy shots, the eye-poppers, to the pros. As I go a little further, you'll discover why. I'm going to tell you about some of the toughest holes in the whole world. And almost all of them lie here in Uncle Sam country. For the sake of your sanity, I hope you never have to play them. Even the great golf stars complain about them.

Let's begin with the Pine Valley course, near Clementon, New Jersey. They have a number five hole that is only a bit over 200 yards and pars out at three. But those 217 yards consist of sand and trees, with a gigantic sand trap straddling the entire fairway. How do you manage to cope with a hole like this? You have to put your first shot *on the green!* If you don't, you're in the rough—and I do mean rough!—or you're on that sandy fairway, which is almost as bad.

The fifth and the fourteenth holes at St. Andrews in Scotland are very long, well over 500 yards, though it isn't this so much that makes them difficult. The fairways seem to be made of grass that takes the bounce away from the ball. Not even the great pros can reach the greens in two shots. You can imagine how many strokes the duffers will take! To add to these hazards, there is usually a stiff Scottish wind blowing, which does its best to blow you into the rough.

Pine Valley has another lulu, its seventh hole. This is

a par five, 570 yards. Bad enough, you must admit, but some sadist has put sand traps all around the green so that it stands out like a black sheep among the white and challenges you to hit a ball that will stay on its smooth, velvety surface.

But you haven't heard the worst. The fairway itself is very narrow and is flanked by forests. There are also two sand traps almost touching each other right across the fairway, challenging you to clear them. If you do clear them, there is then a stretch of sandy soil until you get to the traps that all but smother the poor little green.

I have known good golfers who skip this hole entirely and (generously) give themselves a six. Six! Ha! I'll bet they couldn't do that hole in eight.

There is a 590-yarder at the Baltusrol course in Springfield, New Jersey, which boasts an extremely narrow fairway with rough and woodlands on each side of it. There are sand traps, too, right smack in the middle of the fairway, and more sand traps in front of the green and on one side of it. Of course, beyond the green lies the rough.

Try doing that in par, which is five.

Just in passing, let me say that certain greens—one of them being the eighteenth at the Augusta Country Club in Augusta, Georgia—are wickedly sloped to heighten the despairs of the average golfer. You land on the green in three, but you will have taken four and even five putts before holing out. Greens like this put wrinkles in a golfer's face. Even the great ones are bothered by its curving inclinations.

Merion, in Ardmore, Pennsylvania, has two holes that qualify for the nightmare class. The first one you encounter as you play around is the eleventh. It's only 370-odd yards long, but . . . a little river trickles along in front of the green for a water hazard—you have to walk over a bridge to get to the green—and your drive down the fairway must place you in position for a careful two- or three-iron shot onto the green. If your iron shot is not long enough, your ball goes in the water; if it's too long, you're in the rough beyond the green. And the rough, behind this eleventh hole, consists of a lot of trees and other unmentionable (to a golfer) odds and ends that raise the hackles on a man's head.

Then there is the eighteenth hole, still at Merion. It is 458 yards in length, taking a (ha! ha!) par four. In the middle of the fairway, and over which you must drive, is a stone quarry. I have known strong men to pale when they see what lies before them from the tee. Assuming you get over the quarry, are you home safe? Not on your life! You are still confronted with a lot of fairway, plus sand traps to left and right and ringing the green. Rots of ruck, ferra!

The Augusta National, in Augusta, Georgia, has one hole that ranks with the very worst. It's only 155 yards long, but a small river crosses the fairway a short distance in front of the green, and then between the river and the green is a sand trap. Oh, yeah. There are traps behind the green, too. No woodlands, no forest? Certainly there are, on both sides of the fairway and behind the green.

This same club has another doozy, the eleventh. All you can see as you tee off is a tiny stretch of fairway and trees, trees, trees. There is water to the left of the green and big sand bunkers that wait to eat you and your ball if you set foot in them. You just shoot down the fairway and hope to God that when you blast off your second shot, you won't go anywhere but right onto that sweet green turf. Otherwise, you've had it.

The great pro players often advocate stopping short of the hazard on the fairway so that you can avoid it with your following shot. Gary Player suggests this treatment for the eleventh hole at Augusta. He shoots to the right of the green, thus staying away from that awesome water hole. There are some tough holes that he advocates "attacking," however.

Such a hole is the first at the Augusta Country Club where a sand trap lies to the right of the fairway, but not so far from the tee that it cannot be driven over with reasonable expertise. Once you do this, you are beyond the trap and in line for a following shot that, with any skill at all, should bring you onto the green or close to it, putting at naught the sand trap to its left.

Such advice is excellent, but it is up to the individual player to assess his skills in this regard. If you can drive over a bunker, fine. Do it. If you feel your drive will only carry you into the bunker, then line up your tee shot on that side closest to the bunker and drive away from it, out toward the middle of the fairway.

Much of golf is a question of fine judgments like this.

Always avoid the hazardous shot, unless you are a master of your clubs and strokes. The easiest way is most often the best. Only if you are engaged in match play or are betting for more money than you like to think about is it worth the risk of an all-out, win or go-broke sort of effort.

Speaking of difficult courses, if you are accustomed to playing a fairly tough one and you have a friend who doesn't know the layout, you can take subtle advantage of him by casually forgetting to warn him about trouble spots along the way. If he asks you what's over the brow of the next hill, you can pretend you didn't hear him or be stricken with a violent fit of coughing.

Then if he complains because he overshot the green with a long three-iron blast or put his ball into a little creek that just happened to be meandering across the fairway, you can be all apologies.

"Gosh, Fred," you can say, "I've been so bothered with this hacking cough and have been concentrating on my own problem with my irons that I forgot to tell you about that creek."

Or you can deliberately overclub him when he asks for advice on what club to use for his next shot. When the ball goes about thirty yards past the point where he wanted it to go and winds up in a trap, you can say, "Hell, Fred, you really caught hold of that one. I never figured you to hit one that far from where you were."

You can probably pull this gambit two or three times and get away with it, but don't overdo it, and along about the third time you'll have to tell him ruefully, "Freddie, boy, I've never seen you cream the ball the way you're doing today."

Before I turn away from the subject of tough golf courses, I feel obliged to mention Pebble Beach. This course is located in Pebble Beach, California, and it flanks the Pacific Ocean, above high stone cliffs that add to the mental hazards of an already formidable golf course.

There is a story currently circulating about one golfer who drove off the tee on the eighth hole, rushed to one side to study his angle of flight—and fell into the ocean! This gives you an idea of how a golf architect can make nature work for him.

Playing the kind of psychological golf I am advocating, you might consider any kind of ruse—if you're playing this hole or a similar hole—to get your opponent to shift his position quickly (yell about his line of flight, fall against him as if you were having a dizzy spell) so that he tumbles into the water. A plunge into cold water should really shake him up. In addition, playing in wet clothes and with his feet sloshing around in his golf shoes should really add strokes to his game.

Here's another thing I might mention about this same eighth hole at Pebble Beach. As you tee up your ball (taking due care not to fall into the Pacific), you will find that the fairway disappears at one point. I really mean this. There's a gorge faced by rock cliffs that drives deep into that part of the fairway where you would naturally expect to see grass growing. There is beach and surf below, if you care to step to the edge of that chasm and peer down.

Naturally, if you have nerves of cold steel and a great drive, you can put your ball over that chasm and onto the fairway beyond.

I should advise against it, unless you are a pro.

Be chicken and drive to the left, and as you watch your ball soar high into the air, pray that it will not slice. If you hook your drive, you won't go into that chasm. However, for most of us golfers, the gorge doesn't present too great a problem until we approach our *second* shot. My advice still holds. Hook your shot to the left, and stay on terra firma. There is no more disheartening sound in golf than to hear your ball playing *clickety-clunk* against the walls of that chasm on its way into the Pacific Ocean.

The eighteenth on Pebble Beach flanks the ocean all the way, on the fairway's left. There is rough to the right. Once again, you tee up on the edge of the sea, with all that water on your left just defying you to miss it. There are also a couple of trees *on* the fairway, to add to the fun.

Now, you might figure that after going through all this, you have a right to expect the roll to the green to be smooth and easy. Not on your life! Sand traps surround the green on every side. Like man, you're a nervous wreck when you finally hole in on this one.

I mention all these tough courses with the idea of giving you some more ammunition in your psychological golf warfare. You really should bone up on some of these courses where even the pros sweat to come in close to par. It gives you a perfectly fair advantage.

To your opponent, you mention casually that the last time you played at Pebble Beach (whether you ever have or not makes no difference unless your fellow player knows you've been no nearer Pebble Beach than Kansas City), you took only a six on the eighteenth. You drove straight down the fairway, played an iron shot to the edge of a sand trap, pitched onto the green, and then took three putts to hole out.

Never make your story too good. Your partner just won't believe you. But he might believe you if you throw in that three-putt bit. It adds a certain pinch of truth to add flavor to an otherwise out-and-out whopper.

The result of this will be to make him strain to match this supposedly great play of yours.

You have it made if you travel at all on your job. Nobody can prove that you weren't playing golf at Merion or at Augusta when you last went into Pennsylvania or Georgia. You can even add confidentially that you sneaked away for a day's play, and beg him not to tell your wife, who thinks you worked hard as hell, you poor dear! This, too, adds a bit of verisimilitude.

Then there are what I call the luxury courses. This has nothing to do with whether the courses are tough or easy, but *where* they are. Status is part of golf, and you can lift your status immeasurably when you bring into the casual conversation that the golf course at Tobago, with its traps filled with fine white sand, its grasses greener than you have ever seen them, is the last word in affluent golf playing.

Be sure you have been to Tobago, though. It would never do for your partner to quiz your wife about island golf unless you have really been there. If you have ever been to Jamaica, you might casually say that while you were stopping at the Holiday Inn there, you played over that classy layout designed by Robert Trent Jones.

You can play this game of golf-upmanship very easily by writing to various chambers of commerce, asking for literature about golf courses in faraway places with romantic names, or directly to the great hotel chains who will be only too happy to inundate you with literature about what they have to offer, for a price. By specifying the fact that you are interested in golf, you will also get much verbiage about the pleasure (never the hazards) of knocking a Maxfli or Titleist about on their own courses.

One word of caution: You must never place yourself in a position where it can be proved you were definitely not playing golf on the sun-tipped fairways of Bermuda when you say you were. This is rule number one. Of course, if you ever were in Bermuda, you can just about say what you want, and nobody will be able to disprove it.

In fact, if you travel almost anywhere near a golf course and there isn't a foreign spy trailing you and marking down everywhere you go, you can always add its golf course to your fund of status stories.

Rule number two is: Make very certain there *is* a

golf course at the spot where you say you were playing around in just three over par. Certain exotic places in this world, strange as it may seem, do not possess golf courses.

So be sure before you speak.

Take a trip south into the Carolinas if you want. Visit one of the five magnificent eighteen-hole courses that Pinehurst boasts. No matter if you play. Just drive past one of them, get its flavor, and mention that a millionaire friend of yours invited you to play around with him.

Bits of atmosphere help here. Be sure to get in the narrow lanes that curve back upon themselves, the magnolia trees and the split-rail fences, the slow grandeur of life as it is lived in this southern town. Talk knowledgeably about the racetracks that abound here, the horses and the horse-lovers.

The golf you have or have not played will become almost incidental. Your partner will believe you and will be consumed by jealousy. If only he had ever played at Pinehurst with the rich, seen the azaleas and the dogwoods, putted out in two on that ninth hole! His heart will be filled with envy and his mind with visions of you traipsing around eighteen of the ninety holes the Pinehurst Country Club can boast.

You get in a body blow by mentioning that you have shared martinis with fellow golf enthusiasts at Pinehurst's "Ninety-first Hole," which is the bar. You can also explain, if you want, how James W. Tufts bought five thousand acres of barren land and built a golf course there in 1895. And of how his vision was prophetic and that his family still owns and operates the country club.

Drop a bomb by talking about the Tin Whistle Club. This is a drinking club reserved for about two hundred people at Pinehurst, and got its name from the fact that a tin whistle once hung from a tree and when blown was the signal for bending the elbow in a bit of liquid conviviality.

Invited to down a few with the Tin Whistlers? Of course you were! Who's to prove you weren't? As long as you were in or near Pinehurst at the time, that is.

Or if you've been to the islands, speak of the Tryall Golf and Beach Club at Montego Bay. Montego Bay is in Jamaica. Always check your geography carefully when you begin expounding on these faraway places. There's bound to be some character in the crowd who also has played there. He'll be certain to start asking questions.

Wave away the question with a grin and another statement, such as, "Oh, yes. I know Doctor's Cave Beach—took a dip there after a rough eighteen holes one afternoon. But to get back to that shot I was telling you about. . . ."

There's always a way to put off these nosy Parkers.

You talk about the palm trees that rise like magic wands all over the Tryall course, dappling the lush green grass of the fairway in shifting shadows. Against the green grass and even the lush green of the roughs (which aren't really bad at all) the sand of the traps lie like little jewels. The sea wind blows salt in your nostrils, filling you with *joie de vivre*. Hell! Who couldn't break par under those conditions?

"Did you really break par, Jim?" they will ask.

"Bet I did!"

You will notice how cleverly you are hedging here. You are not saying outright that you broke par. In a sense, you are wondering if they want to bet you on whether you did or not. But don't ask it like a question. Say it like a man, chin up and defying the world. Remember the exclamation point in that sentence. It's important.

If you really want to wow 'em, just say "Mo Bay" for Montego Bay. It will make you sound like a native. Again a warning: If you have never been close to Jamaica, forget the Montego Bay bit. Instead, concentrate your attentions on a course closer to home. Invite your wife out for a Sunday drive and dinner at some glamorous spot that just happens to be situated not far from a status golf course. After she faints and you have revived her, take your drive. Be sure to go past the golf course very slowly. Your wife will still be in a mild state of shock and will permit this with an indulgent smile.

Let's say you choose Fairfield County in Connecticut. This isn't too hard to reach from almost anywhere in the metropolitan New York area, or even from New Jersey. Fairfield County is affluent, man. Many of its plush businessmen go to New York by helicopter. It has a Gold Coast, and it also requires you to build on a minimum of two acres. It is rich, by any standard.

And it has, naturally enough, status golf clubs.

Your wife will be dazzled by the idea of dining at the Red Barn or perhaps Silvermine. These very luxurious eateries are not too far from, say, the Wee Burn or the Country Club of Fairfield.

So you drive past Wee Burn or the Country Club of Fairfield. Pick whichever one you want. Get out of the car to stretch your legs and absorb some of the local color of the course. Even go so far as to memorize a particular hole, its bunkers, the rough, the fairway, the location of the green. Do this while you are stretching your legs. Your wife may even walk with you, since she should be in a pretty good mood.

Now get back in your car, give your wife a little kiss to keep her happy, and plan your psychological warfare next time you play with Fred. You'll find that your dinner will taste better, the wine ever so much mellower. Your wife will be more beautiful.

Next time you play golf, you will discourse knowingly on the hole you have memorized; you will explain carefully because you have already gone over it, stroke by stroke in your head, how you broke par on it. A business friend invited you to play the course, or some such thing. Your fellow player won't care about that. What he wants to know is what was the course like, how big were its traps, how bad the roughs.

You tell him, from your own observation.

If you ever get to Banff, where the terrain is something out of a travelogue booklet, you will play the golf course there which fashions its fairways alongside Spray

River. This is always good for a bit of golf-upmanship, particularly when you bring in the Royal Canadian Northwest Mounties, who are located very close by.

There are lush spots like this all over the world.

All you have to do is find a golf course for the very rich near your home, or within a good day's driving, with a name restaurant to be stopped at with your wife or current girlfriend, and you have reloaded your golf grabbag of psychological put-ons.

It will help your game, too, to go to a real golf tournament where you can see the big-name players socking the ball as you wish you could, and so do I. There are tournaments at golf clubs near you, no matter where you live.

One such tournament around my neck of the woods is the Westchester Classic. The Westchester Country Club, in Rye, New York, has two courses that cater to the affluent of our society. No, I am not a member. But I can go and look, even as you. And when I am told that the amount of money to be won at this tournament is in the neighborhood of a quarter of a million dollars, I look with very big eyes, indeed.

Oak trees, old and stately, line the fairways. There is an air of money all about. The broad tile terraces, the imposing clubhouse, the fine restaurant, all bear the aura of the glamour decades of the past. Soak up this atmosphere when you go to Westchester. It helps, in some indefinable way, when you say that you saw Julius Boros score a birdie on the famous West course or Tommy Armour shoot an eagle. (A birdie, for you non-golfers, is one stroke under par. An eagle is two strokes under par, for any particular hole. It can be done, if you are good enough. Even I have made a birdie once or twice, when I was very lucky.)

However, the main thing to emphasize here is not scoring, but association. You have seen Arnie Palmer drive; you have watched Jack Nicklaus hammer a two-iron all the way onto the green. In some way that even long-time golfers cannot explain, you will have added a touch of their magic to your character, especially when you mention in a casual way that by such observation, you have bettered your own game. You are giving your opponent food to feed his worriment.

And that's the name of the game. My game, anyhow. And maybe yours.

4

Handicaps and Other Hazards

One of the finest ways ever devised by the mind of man to psych your opponent is the golf handicap. Now, this doesn't mean that you get to swing your clubs with two hands while your opponent uses only one. Actually, the great moving-picture magnate Will Fox really played golf using only one arm for his swing and putts. There may have been others. I know a lot of players who feel they play that way even when both hands are involved.

No, the handicap I am referring to is your golf handicap. It works this way. There are all varieties of golfers. At the very top we have men like Jack Nicklaus, Arnie Palmer, Lee Trevino, Billy Casper, and a host of other professionals who make upward of several hundred thousand dollars a year by playing golf. These are the awe-inspiring professionals. Many of them teach golf at a country club, for every country club has its pro.

These demigods will shoot near or below par every time they traipse around a golf course. Par is not a bad word to them—it's just something they ignore. If par on a course is 72, most of them will shoot 65 to—on a bad day—75. They are masters of themselves, their clubs, the ball, and the many courses on which they play.

For a great many people, 80 or even 90 is a damn good score.

Then there are the others, even you and I, who feel they have just about mastered the game when their score dips below that magical 100 mark. For the most part, they play in four-ball groups, erroneously called foursomes, in which four good men and true get together for a round on a sunny day. These foursomes can be mixed, when women play with men—golf, I'm talking about—and go around the course usually with the one woman and a man playing against the other woman and a man. There are other varieties of match-ups that will be dealt with in the proper time.

Now obviously, all these players do not tackle golf with the same amount of skill. There are always the gifted ones, among whom I will number the men and women whose usual score is 80. Now, par being 72, a score of 80 is obviously above par. This is never given

as a handicap. Always a few strokes are deducted. So an 80 player has a handicap of 7 or thereabouts. *

Another player shoots 100 day in and day out, always allowing for those times that happen unto the best of us, when for some reason or another anything we tackle goes bad, and the normally 100 player shoots 115 or— yes, it does happen—a ghastly 120. But his normal score is 100. His handicap then becomes about 24. The whole idea behind this is that when the 100-stroke player gets to tangle with the 80-stroke man, they can have a reasonably close game.

And therein lies the danger.

Assume Charley Smith is the man with the low score, and Eddie Baxter plays in the low 100's. They meet on a bright morning in May, the wind is inconsequential, and both men are in a betting mood.

"Your handicap's twenty-four, right, Eddie?" asks good old Charley, scenting money in his wallet. Eddie is loaded; there's no harm in taking a couple of twenties from him. It'll help pay for that mink coat Myrtle wants.

"Twenty-four. Right," says Eddie, grinning.

"Ten a hole?" asks Charley casually.

---

* Handicapping is a complicated procedure that involves selecting a player's ten best rounds of his last twenty to reach an average score which is then compared against a handicap differential chart. However, for the purposes of this book, we will assume that the handicap equals about 85 percent of the difference between the course rating and a player's actual average score over a selected number of rounds. Actually, a course may be a par 72, but its course rating could be 70.5, which means that it plays easier than the par listed on the scorecard.

Ten it is, and Charley drives off, a good 200-yarder straight down the fairway. He picks up his tee, gestures magnanimously to Eddie, and steps back to give Eddie room to swing.

Eddie slams a nice drive, 180 yards in length. Thus Eddie shoots first when they reach his ball. The man whose lie is farthest from the hole always goes first. Eddie then slams a three-iron shot about a hundred yards.

Charley scowls. He shoots, a fine iron shot that carries him well beyond our duffer named Eddie. But Eddie is not out of it. He proceeds to hit a nine-iron close to the green.

This first hole is a par four. Charley always does it in four. It has become routine. He lays his third shot right on the green. One putt—if he sinks it—will give him par.

Eddie chips onto the green, very near the cup. A lucky shot, for him. He damn well will sink his putt unless he gets a fit of the funkies. And Eddie doesn't look anything but healthy and happy.

Charley presses, missing his putt.

Eddie sinks his putt.

Each man has scored a five on the first hole. But—and here is the hidden danger of the handicap—Eddie is now ahead of Charley. Remember, if Eddie shoots 100, with his 24-stroke handicap, he will score a net 76. However, since Charley, at 80, has approximately a 7-stroke handicap, he must give Eddie 17 strokes, or the difference between their respective handicaps. But there are four par-three holes on each course, and strokes are usually not given on short holes, so Charley would likely give Eddie only 13 strokes—a stroke on every hole except the par threes and the easiest of the par fours.*

They keep on playing. Charley begins to press more and more. It is a strange thing about the game of golf, but the internal pressure can make a man do very rash things, like taking three strokes in a single sand trap, when he is mad at his fellow player, at himself and his game, at the course itself.

"Are you sure your handicap is twenty-four?" Charley asks suspiciously after a time.

"Ask the club steward," Eddie says.

Eddie is relaxed and confident; he has no reputation to maintain. The sun is shining, and all's right with his little world. Meanwhile, the pressures are building inside Charley Smith.

For the first nine holes, Charley shoots a 45. Not good, for him, but he is not on top of his game today. Eddie has shot a 50. If they are involved in medal play (the match is governed by individual holes won, not by the overall score) and Eddie's *net* scores on holes has enabled him to beat Charley on three holes, Charley then owes Eddie thirty bucks already.

Not so good, hey?

So what happens? Why, Charley begins to press even

---

* Strokes are given on the most difficult holes. For example, if Eddie were getting only 5 strokes from Charlie, Eddie would get a stroke on each of the five most difficult holes as rated on the score card, so that if hole number one were rated the most difficult, Eddie's 5 would give him a net 4, thus meaning he has won that hole in medal play.

more. He has to make back that fifty iron men! Even if
he plays Eddie even (or better than even to make up
for the strokes he must give Eddie) on the last nine
holes, he's still out money.

When a golfer presses, his game goes haywire. His
drives slice, his iron shots hook, he walks around in the
rough looking for lost balls, he may even blast a ball
into a lake. He is allowed to replace the ball, but it costs
him a stroke.

Eddie, without a worry in the world, just plays his
so-so game. That old devil handicap is riding with him
at every swing of his club. Eddie winds up with an
even 100, right on handicap target. Charley, a far better
player, scores a 92. He is lucky to keep Eddie from winning any more holes and succeeds in topping his friend
on two holes so that he winds up by owing ten dollars.

He pays the ten, not happily, and runs to see the
club steward. Indeed, Edward Thomas Baxter *does*
have a 24 handicap.

The whole trouble was, Charley started thinking
about Eddie's handicap and what he would have to do
to take him. When Eddie just kept moving around the
course, neither brilliant nor bad, it affected good old
Charley. He wasn't winning the way he should have
been winning, which made him play not as well as he
should, which, in turn, only added to his woes.

He was playing the handicap, not Eddie.

This handicap disconcerts almost all good golfers
who think they should rack up their opposition. It puts
strokes on their scorecards because it takes away their

concentration and, thus, their efficiency. Had Charley played his normal game and scored an 80, he might have won fifty dollars from Eddie.

I have known more people to blow sky-high because of this handicap business than would be believed. It gets inside a man or woman, it makes them suspicious, and they begin to ask themselves, "Is his handicap really twenty-four? I'll bet he's lying; it's only sixteen." And after the opponent merrily socks his ball here and there with his normal inefficiency but managing to stay close to his handicap performance, the low-handicap man does slow burn after slow burn, always convinced he is being gulled, for some reason or another, until he winds up the loser in the match.

This handicap is especially serious at the time of the club championships. Your hardened veteran will play his game, and with any luck at all, have a good stab at the big silver cup and the chance to have his name inscribed on the plaque that hangs in the bar as the winner for the year. If he doesn't worry about the handicaps, that is. Otherwise, forget about his chances. Besides, the high-handicap golfer can always have a good day and play way over his head, and if he is getting a lot of strokes from a better player, he can really wind up reaming the other guy.

You will have noted by now that this game of golf is almost all psychology. Each man plays his own game against himself. His opponent is not as important as you might think, unless that opponent is playing a psychological game as well as a physical one. More on this in subsequent pages. It's very important, so keep it in mind.

Psychological warfare can be added to your handicap very neatly if your opponent is one of those thick-skinned individuals who don't realize what a weapon your twenty-stroke handicap can be. Maybe you are only playing for a dollar a stroke, and your opponent is already five ahead of you.

So as you walk off the fifth tee together, you say casually, "Jim, I sure am glad I have a twenty-stroke advantage over you, or I'd really be down in the dumps."

"Twenty strokes?" he will ask in an incredulous tone of voice.

"Count 'em. Twenty."

If he doesn't say anything, you walk on for another ten yards before you speak. But you always mention this one more time, especially before he has taken his next shot. Then you say, "That's a lot of strokes, all right."

There isn't any need to say anything more. Not for a while, anyhow. You have planted the idea in his mind. He cannot help but be thinking about that twenty-stroke advantage you have. If he shoots to a ten handicap, he'll be thinking that he's got to shoot that much better than you to break even.

Believe me, he will be thinking of this as he addresses his ball for the next shot. His brain will be whispering, "Bill had ten strokes on me before I even began. Ten strokes. My God! I've got to make every shot count!"

Ten to one he slices one into the rough.

You'll win your five back and five more in hardly any time at all as long as you keep applying the pressure with an occasional comment like, "Boy, you're a great golfer, Jim. I'm not in your class. Not at all. I sure am glad I have those ten strokes to fall back on."

What you're doing here is building up his ego. He admits he's a fine golfer to begin with, and what you're doing is making him realize it all the more. He has to prove it to you, and to himself. The urge to show off will become irresistible. He will slam the next drive and thereby lose accuracy and go off the fairway, or maybe even shank the ball so it goes off at a sharp tangent to the right and winds up next to a tree. Either way, you're as good as a stroke ahead of him already.

After a time, being a good golfer, he will settle down.

This is when you apply the needle a little more.

"Let's see, now," you murmur as you both advance on the ninth green. "You owe me one dollar. Not bad for a duffer like me, hey?"

Even if you're wrong, say it.

Your opponent will stop and check his scorecard and yours, and if he does owe you that one buck, he'll start to press like crazy to make it up. And he will commit mistakes, giving you your chance to make a killing. If he doesn't owe you a dollar, but you owe him two, this will have taken his mind off his game and his next shot just long enough for him to flub his putt and give you the opportunity to win back one or more of those bucks you already owe him.

This must not be overdone. Never be obvious. If he suspects what you're trying to do, he will be on his guard against it. You never have to say very much; all you need to do is give him the idea about your handicap. Don't let him forget it, but don't keep repeating it. His own mind will do that, especially when he's in a difficult lie and knows he can't afford extra strokes.

Never, under any circumstances, get your opponent mad at your handicap. Let him get mad at himself, not at you. Always remember, he must hit his ball perfectly to get the perfect shot he needs. If he gets mad enough, he may very well be able to add to his powers of concentration. So don't make him angry. Just keep him worried.

Worry can accomplish a lot, because it is a mental phenomenon churning inside the player. Worry causes him to doubt himself, which leads him, in turn, to doubt his clubs, his golf ball, his ability to clear the water hazard or avoid the sand traps. And when this happens, nine times out of ten he will do exactly what he wants most to avoid, and so add to his score. Never downgrade your opponent. Flatter him, instead. Vanity is a curse, and what man can resist a statement like this: "That was a terrific shot, old boy! I want to study your swing on your next one, to see how a really good player does it."

This will make him think about the placement of his hands about the shaft—called the grip—about his stance and whether his head is placed correctly so that he can keep his eye on the ball while he is hitting it, and a thousand and one other things. Instead of concentrating just on hitting the ball correctly, his mind is wandering. And when his mind wanders, so will his ball.

There is a fine art to this flattery. It cannot be overdone, or it will sound false. Your voice has to have the right inflection, the correct tone. Say it as though you really mean it.

Try it out a little at a time, just to test the results. Some players will actually go to pieces if you're subtle about it. The main idea is to keep them thinking about themselves and the quality of their own game, while you hook and slice around the course as merrily as you can.

Being a duffer, nobody expects *you* to make good shots all the time. There's no pressure on you. But keep applying it to the other guy.

The following ploy is always good for a few strokes: "Jim, you have too high a handicap. I'll bet you could play the club pro just about even." And watch how he'll try to justify your high regard of him. By playing worse than you do, usually.

I would never tell an opponent he has too low a handicap. This makes a person angry and may well cause him to play better than he knows how.

Remember, now. Flattery, first of all, but don't ladle it on too heavily. Then a reminder, every so often, that your handicap is greater than his. Keep him thinking about these things, about his correct stance and the proper grip, and you'll be drinking martinis at his expense in the club bar after the game.

Thanks to that little old handicap!

5

To Caddy or to Cart?

Your normal eighteen-hole golf course comprises about four miles of real estate. If you walk it, you will have been on your legs for about five hours, driving, hitting your irons, pitching into or over or out of sand traps, and putting. Putting means you will be bending over about forty times if you are a reasonably good golfer.

This is excellent exercise. Doctors have recommended that patients take up golf to get the exercise it gives. Walking is good for patients with heart trouble. Hell, it's good for all of us, and most especially for guys and gals who sit on their rumps five days a week behind a desk.

You are out in the open air; you are moving almost all the muscles of your body. At the finish of your eigh-

teen holes, assuming you have not played such an awful game that your energy is depleted by your mental
state, you will have the glow of health that all of us
would like to have.

Now, then, this presents a problem.

Are you physically able to carry your golf bag with
all the various clubs it contains? In my younger days
I did this, much to the disgust of the caddy master and
the caddies who may or may not have looked upon me
as a soft touch. But I got a lot of exercise.

If you are like most of us, beginning to get a bit
soft, the idea of lugging thirty-odd pounds of equipment around with you along four miles of fairways,
greens, and roughs, whenever you feel the urge to
play golf, becomes somewhat distasteful. For you, there
is always the caddy.

A caddy is a person who carries your golf bag, feeds
you your clubs when you ask for them, and lifts the
pin out of the cup when that great shot you have hit
seems to be on its way home. He will also, upon re-
quest, furnish advice as to which club to use in any
given situation.

For all this, you will pay a fee. And give him a tip.
There are caddies, and caddies. Some are expert golfers; others couldn't care less about the game. They are
in this for the money they will make and not because
they give a hoot about whether you beat Eddie Baxter
or Charley Smith.

The top pros have their own special caddies. These
men travel the professional circuit with them; they

know their clients as you know the foibles of your wife or children. Does Creamy Carolan know that Arnie Palmer has a temper? He sure does. And does Angelo Argea know that Jack Nicklaus has a fault in his back-swing and is on the lookout for it? Of course he does, and is. These caddies are professionals themselves, and they are paid handsomely, because they help the pros stay on top of their game.

For most of us, a caddy is just a face, somebody who does the menial work of holding the golf bag over his shoulder and is always there with it when you walk up to your ball. He is going to expect a tip for these services, which is only right and fair. And you will be glad to tip him when you come to the end of the eighteenth hole if he actually contributes something to your game.

I suggest you try him out on the very first hole. Might as well learn if he will be a help or a hindrance, right away.

You will say, looking at the lie of your drive, off to one side of the fairway, "Ought I use a three-wood or a two-iron, caddy?"

If he gets a glassy look in his eyes and maybe shrugs his shoulders, I wouldn't count on any advice from him for the rest of the day. Be satisfied with the fact that the golf-bag strap is chafing his shoulder, not yours, and that if the time comes when you need somebody who will watch the pin as you chip in from the fringe of the green without having to putt, it will be he who will be standing there, ready to assist in your hour of triumph.

It might be a good idea to make friends with your caddy at the first opportunity, too. I have known players who will ask their golf helpers, "Do you have good eyesight?"

And if they are men with a keen eye for a buck but are able to wink at the little foibles of all golfers, they will say, "I don't know how to add, if that's what you mean."

"It means a ten spot for you," you mutter in an aside.

They can add that much, believe me.

This comes in very handy on the fifth hole, for instance, when you take an extra swing in the rough but don't report it. You lie, and your caddy will swear to it, like a gentleman.

There are some caddies who will insist upon reporting your score in a loud voice, however, as you move from the green to the next tee. These are few and far apart, happily. However, they must be dealt with summarily.

If your caddy does say you took a five and not that four you so cheerfully reported, you must turn to him in surprise and ask, "A five, caddy? Now what stroke did I leave off?"

And when he tells you about the swing in the rough, you can act injured and maintain it was only a practice swing. Then you add dramatically, taking out your scorecard and changing the four to a five, "I certainly don't want to cheat anybody. If my caddy thought it was a real swing, I'm going to put it down. No, no, Charley, I play a fair, honest game. I won't have it said that I cheated anybody."

This will make everyone think you are an honest player.

Naturally, you will murmur to your caddy *sotto voce,* "Do you or do you not want a good tip, young man?"

Say this when you are damn sure nobody can hear you except the caddy. If he's as smart as all the other caddies I have known, he will blink and grin a little shamefacedly and say something like, "Sorry about that extra stroke, sir. I didn't know it was a practice swing. It won't happen again."

You test him out again on the seventh. Your ball, unfortunately, lies in the rough because you have sliced your driver. It is an especially bad lie because there are a couple of trees right in front of it. You know the ball is bound to hit one of those trees no matter how you play it, unless you waste a shot and tap it sideways out into the nearest patch of fairway.

So you pretend you don't see it and give it a good kick with your foot while making believe you're looking for it. The ball bounces away and comes to rest in a pretty good lie, the rough being what it is.

Looking your caddy right in the eye, you say, "I suppose I ought to replace the ball. I didn't see where it was."

If he nods and looks as if you had better replace it, you give him up as a bad proposition. Forget him and save money on your tip.

But if he says something like, "Kick it? I didn't see you do that!"—why, then, you know he's on your side all the way to the nineteenth hole. You will have to pay for this kind of service, so be generous with your tipping.

And remember his face. You may have need of him at a later date. You and he work well over the course. All this is well worth the investment of a good tip, especially if you are the sort of player who likes to sweeten his game with a side bet or two or three. You can possibly make enough money from your fellow players so that the tip to your caddy becomes insignificant.

There are other advantages to be gained when there is a rapport between you and your caddy. If he's as smart as the caddies I know, he will have hurried ahead of you and surreptitiously moved your ball to a better lie in the rough on his own initiative. He will do this skillfully, of course, when nobody is watching him, while pretending to hunt for a ball he knows very well isn't lost.

Next time you play, ask for him.

Usually, when he sees you approaching the caddy master, he will be there as big as life, with a huge grin. You and he are partners in golf crime, and well he knows it.

A great many golf professionals were caddies before they grew up and took to the pro circuits. If you are fortunate enough to get yourself one of these budding geniuses, always pay heed to his advice about the way to play a hole or the proper club to use when making a shot. Chances are he can go around the course in par, or maybe even under it. He knows it as well as does the golf pro, or perhaps even better. He has tried the shots you are thinking of attempting, and from his study of you (all caddies study you, no matter what they do or say) he will know at once whether you can bring that particular shot off. So do what he says.

A great many caddies will not offer advice unless it is specifically requested. They are playing a game, too. They are assessing you, even as you are assessing them. Sometimes they will offer advice in a guarded way, to learn your reaction.

If you brush them off in your supposedly greater wisdom, they will clam up for the rest of the round. But if you flash them a friendly smile or speak a word of thanks, they will allow that maybe you're a regular guy and help you with a word of caution now and again.

If your caddy suggests hitting your tee shot to the left to avoid the trees on that side of the fairway, do it. He has probably learned this the hard way. If he tells you to use a spoon when you were thinking of a two-iron, it's because he has seen that you can handle woods better than you do irons.

But perhaps you are not interested in having a caddy at your elbow as you wend your way around the course. There are wheeled carts you can rent for the day in which to place your golf clubs and any other accessories you may need to go a round, and you either wheel them before you or drag them in your wake as you move from hole to hole.

These little carriers have certain advantages. They will not be able to watch as you go haywire in that sand trap and take five strokes. Your caddy will be thinking that you are the worst golfer he has ever seen (or you will convince yourself that this is what he is thinking as you whack away at that pesky ball in the middle of all that sand), but your golf cart stands mute and dumb at the edge of the bunker, without eyes to see your many mistakes or ears to hear your profanity.

Neither do you have to tip them. All you do is pay a fee for their use.

Then there are the golfmobiles. These are little motor carts, propelled by electricity or gasoline, in which you sit with your golf clubs and drive yourself around the course. The electric carts run quietly and efficiently. The gas carts are apt to be faster but are noisy and, like cars, give off exhaust fumes. Some are completely open to the sun, others have surrey tops to provide a measure of shade, and at some clubs you'll even find carts with windshields to protect you against wind and rain. They all accommodate two people and cruise along at a slightly better speed than a fast walk.

One of the first such machines I ever heard of was the linksmobile ordered by Curtis W. Willcock when his doctor advised him to give up golf. Willcock had the linksmobile made to his order and played around his course in it.

Not all of us are so rich. We must make do with the electric or gas carts that are furnished by the country club or golf links to which we belong.

However, a motorized cart can be made to serve a purpose in the psychological warfare that you are always waging with your fellow players. I know of one man who has a particularly queasy stomach and who is reduced to a pale, shaking hulk when he is conducted over the course by some heartless wretch who is playing against him.

These men will run to get behind the wheel and never heed the pleas of Nervous Ned, as we shall call him. These players will take that golfmobile over the roughest terrain they can find. They rejoice over those fairways that are fairly hilly. They take those hills at a fast clip that equates them with the thank-you-ma'ams we all knew when we used to go sleigh riding in the wintertime.

The dips and rises of that cart actually make Nervous Ned sick. His opponent apologizes profusely as he bumps and bounces and turns sharply and recklessly in the rough, always managing to bite his lip to hide a big grin when Ned stumbles weakly from the cart to try to hit his ball. His stomach is so tied up in knots that he always adds two or three strokes on every hole.

The idea, of course, is to try to do all the driving. Use quick starts and stops, take all turns sharply, and aim for every bump or depression in the rough, so that your opponent's insides never get a chance to settle. And you can always state casually that you have to know how to handle those contraptions, then tell the story of a friend who was careless on a slope and got tossed out of his cart breaking two ribs, and an arm. A tale like this is sure to add a little emotional tension to the physical shaking up your opponent is getting.

When Nervous Ned sometimes protests at the constant travel in the rough, as he has been known to do on more than one occasion, the driver can always say, "The fairways are a little soft from all that rain we had this week, and I don't want to mark them up. So we'll take a little detour over these bunkers and through this patch of rocky ground."

His friends study the terrain of these roughs for particularly bumpy ground, believe me. Sometimes I get the feeling that they know the roughs far better than they know the fairways.

Now, when Ned becomes too insistent, the driver will often go so far as to run over Ned's ball, blaming supposedly faulty brakes, wedging it deep into the ground where Ned will have to use a nine-iron to get it out rather than the normal spoon or three-iron shot that he had planned on using. Naturally, this adds more strokes than usual to his game.

I have been told on good authority that these carts can also be used for a little smooching when one is playing golf with a particularly desirable female in a mixed twosome or foursome. The technique used here is that you drive deep into the rough, then wend your way with the golf cart and your pretty opponent or partner as far into the woods as necessary.

You now stop and say, "Why don't we hunt for the ball from here, you gorgeous creature?"

However, I must warn the reader that such conduct is frowned upon by true golfers. A golf course is for golf *only!*

If you are a reasonably good golfer and are honestly interested in improving your score, I would advise that you hire a caddy. He may help you improve your game.

If you're a real duffer and want as few people as possible to see those whiffs and tops, the shanked balls and the slices, to say nothing of the hooks that may be in a class by themselves, then you don't want a caddy anywhere within viewing distance. For you, I suggest the golf hand cart. The expense is minimal, the cart will be holding the weight of your clubs and bag, and it will never remind you about the sand trap on the third. It has a handle you can grab without too much trouble, and its wheels roll along silently as you pull it behind you. It's almost as if you were out for a walk, with an occasional pause to belt that pesky ball.

Personally, I feel that a golf course should be walked over. It is excellent exercise, and in this day and age we all need as much exercise as we can get. So hire either a caddy or a hand cart.

I realize that there are people to whom walking is anathema. For these, I say, hire a motorized cart. Drive or be driven over the four miles, getting out to drive or use your irons. At least, you're out in the open air, and that's a good thing.

Another point to consider is that many golfers, being very busy people, are often hard-pressed for time. Let's say you have a couple of hours to spare. With an electric or gasoline golf cart you can go around your favorite course in that length of time and still keep your date with the blonde or attend the dinner-dance your wife insists upon being seen at. To such as these, the golfmobile is like manna from heaven.

Before closing out the discussion of golf carts, I must mention a new and recent innovation at some of the plusher clubs—the automatic cart that follows the player at a distance of a few feet. This cart resembles a small dune buggy and holds one golf bag. The player wears a special belt equipped with an electronic button arrangement that is strapped to his waist with the controls in the back. As the player moves, the cart follows him at a regulated distance. However, you must be careful to shut off the controls before walking into a sand trap or a water hazard, or the cart will follow you.

A subtle psychological ploy you might use on your opponent if you elect this kind of contraption is to try to distract him with conversation or a locker-room tale while he's walking into a trap or close to a pond so that the cart waltzes into the hazard before he can switch off the controls. If the cart tips over and his golf bag falls into the sand or the water, it could upset your "friend" long enough to have him bolo a couple of shots and throw him into an emotional tizzy.

But caddy or hand cart or motorized cart or electronic buggy—whichever it shall be—is up to your own individual needs and enjoyment. Think about it, study your budding paunch, deliberate on your state of health, and then make your decision. And use whichever you choose as part of your psychological campaign in playing dirty golf.

6

Four-Balls, Two-Balls,
and Mixed Foursomes

Golf is a social game. By this I mean that you normally play it with other human beings. Your neighbor, perhaps, or your neighbor and his wife with you and your wife. For wife you may read girlfriend, if neither player is married.

The two-ball game, when two men or two women play each other, is usually a far more grim experience than golf when it is played with members of the opposite sex. The stag game often degenerates into a match of frayed nerves, curt words, and glances that can kill at more than six paces. When two women go over the course together and there is any rivalry between them at all, very much the same thing occurs. Sometimes, even more so.

Two men, when they go walking over the links, are, more often than not, friendly enemies. Each is out to show the other he can score lower than his buddy. To prove this, a man will stoop, at times, to an ethical code upon which he would frown with distaste in any other game or even in business.

This is where psychological warfare truly touches the peaks.

A player will often go to bed early (yeah, even on a Saturday night). He will be up earlier and with more pep in his step than on weekdays when he goes to the office on the daily business round. It is best for his wife to stay in bed on such mornings. Her mate will not be at his best. He will be too worried about the upcoming trials—his putting game or his iron play or perhaps that double sand trap that lies across the fairway on the eleventh hole and that he can never seem to clear without the loss of at least two strokes—to be in a friendly mood.

He may or may not eat.

Now, I always enjoy a good breakfast before I go out to play eighteen holes. By the time I reach the first tee, that breakfast will be pleasantly settled, ready to furnish me with the energy needed to play golf and psych myself and my partner around the links. It is bad enough to be on the eleventh green and feel your stomach tying itself in knots at the prospect of a twenty-foot putt without having already ill-treated your stomach by refusing it the only thing it really wants out of life: food.

So I eat well for starters. At least, my insides won't

have *that* to complain about. Scrambled eggs, toast, and coffee always provide me with the necessary fuel. If it's a brisk fall or spring day, I cajole my mate into making me some pancake batter the night before so I can enjoy griddle cakes with sausage before I set foot outside the house.

I also drink several cups of coffee. Coffee warms the body, sets my blood to stirring, and assures me that all will be well with my game on this fine day.

Some players I know refuse to eat breakfast. This renders them utterly unsociable by the time they reach the tenth green. It also, I suspect, reduces their energy because they begin to lag thereabouts. Their drives are not so long; their putts are slightly off.

I encourage my opponents to fast. It's part of my golf game, which means that if I can con some poor sucker into tottering around the course on the last five or six holes by talking him into not eating anything since dinnertime the night before, I can maybe make up in strokes what I have lost in the early going.

An empty stomach also means that when you finally reach the club bar, a martini or a manhattan will produce an effect like a depth bomb in your insides. These are the golfers who have to call their wives to come and get them.

But with a full breakfast under your belt, you can go out and give that ball a good, healthy whack. You aren't worrying about how you'll feel, come the sixteenth tee. You may even feel so good after a fine breakfast that you'll go upstairs where your wife is wisely curled up in bed and give her a good-bye kiss, at which she will sleepily wish you good luck. This makes your wife realize you really love her and scores brownie points in your marital relations.

It is very smart at this time to make sure you have your good-luck charm in your golf bag. If you don't have one, invent it.

I am reminded of the story they tell about Gene Sarazen and how he always attributed his success at winning the first Masters Tournament he had ever entered, held on the Augusta National, to a good-luck ring that had been given him by a friend. Of course, it was his superb play that won it, but the ring didn't hurt. Maybe it gave him that little extra measure of confidence just when he needed it most. I like to think so.

Be that as it may, I suggest that you obtain a good-luck object. It needn't be anything more or less than an old cap, a neckerchief, a rabbit's foot, an old battered club. Anything at all.

It will help you if you really do have good luck with it, but even if you don't, you can always use it against your opponent.

You lift the half-dollar (we'll say) out of your pocket right when you need it most, to sink a twelve-footer. You toss the coin in the air, catch it, and remark, "This is the time I need you, old buddy!"

You try to sink the putt. If you do happen to do just that, you will have badly shattered your opponent. You have a good-luck symbol working for you. He doesn't, and it will worry him. Just enough, let's hope.

If you don't sink the putt, you say, "Well, that 1923 half-dollar can't be expected to do it all the time."

Then, very cheerfully (never show dismay at a moment like this), you turn a smiling face to your opponent and murmur, "Nine times out of ten, it really does work for me."

He will think about that for the rest of the game. He will wait for you to drag out that half a buck, and if you ever should sink that putt or hit that wonderful two-iron shot onto the green, he will be convinced.

A note on sartorial elegance will fit in nicely here. A very colorful sweater or a psychedelic sort of shirt, if you can ignore it and play your normal game, may be something of a weapon in the psychology department, especially if you are playing against a gentleman who believes in a drab sport shirt and plain sweater as the proper links attire.

If something bright and colorful bothers you, however, if you are more conscious of the socks you wear than of the socks you give the ball, ignore this advice. The main idea of the game is to make your opponent uncomfortable, not you. But sometimes a paisley-print knit shirt will so distract your opponent, especially if you stand where he can't help but notice it, when he is in the middle of a swing, that he will commit a few bad blunders. You don't have to move, even. Just make sure you're where his eye—which should be on the ball—is on your shirt.

It helps if a wind is blowing. The wind will ruffle the shirt, sort of waggle all those wild colors, so that it will seem as if somebody is wigwagging with signal flags on the edge of your opponent's peripheral vision.

There are numerous other gambits you can practice

that can throw your opponent off stride. You might try jingling some coins in your pocket until the last second or two before he lunges at his tee shot. He's bound to hear that infernal jingling, and the noise will creep in just enough to take some of the edge off his concentration.

You might try blowing your nose while he's going into his preliminary waggle or do a little discreet humming under your breath, then cut it off at the last minute and murmur an apology, "Oops, sorry, Fred. I didn't realize you were ready to hit." You can substitute a belch or a cough for a nose-blowing session, but do it with finesse. Of course, you can't do these things too often. You've got to be cute about it.

Also, you can pretend you notice something about the guy's stance or his practice swing and stop him just as he's about to go into his backswing. "Oh, Fred, sorry —but I noticed you took an awful fast backswing. Better slow it up." Or: "Fred, you've got your feet very far apart. It's going to keep you from pivoting. Didn't mean to interrupt—but I don't want you to rush your shot." Not much!

If Fred's a reasonably nice chap, he'll grin a little tightly and murmur his thanks and start all over again. Hopefully, you've upset his rhythm, and he'll slice or hook his drive.

Here's another great idea: During the first nine holes of an important match you might routinely concede close putts to your opponent until he is so lulled by picking up the ball without putting out that you can really shake him up suddenly on the tenth hole when he putts the ball within a foot of the cup, looks to you for a nod of concession, and you reward him with a blank stare. Realizing he's got to stroke that ball into the cup, he'll tighten up, sweat a little, and nine times out of ten push the ball past the hole. Walter (the Haig) Hagen, famous for his psychological warfare in golf, pulled this stunt on Leo Diegel in the final round of the 1926 P.G.A. tourney played in Salisbury, Long Island, and wound up taking the title.

Another ploy used by the Haig on the putting green was to unnerve his opponent by making light of his own long putts. The trick was particularly effective if Hagen had a much longer putt than the other fellow. He would suddenly start to laugh and keep on chuckling until his opponent asked him what was funny. Hagen would then casually mention that he was thinking how much tougher the other fellow's shot was going to look after he'd sunk his longer shot. Time and again the Haig would hole out from five or six feet while the other player—only inches away—would flub his putt and lose the hole.

Accordingly, if you've got any kind of putting ability, you might try this bit of psychological maneuvering. Of course, it's not likely to work if you miss your shot and push it three feet past the cup.

All these little hints can be useful in playing four-ball foursomes, too, which is when you're playing a round with three other guys. Just be sure you don't try them when your partner, if you're playing partners, is addressing the ball. You want to give *him* all the help you can.

The mixed foursome is a cat of another color. Here, you and a man friend are playing golf with two ladies. They may or may not be wives.

Always flatter your opposing female.

If your wife is going around the links with you, make damn sure she knows in advance about this bit of psychology. It won't do at all to win the match and have the little woman in a towering rage because of all the attention you've been paying to Myrtle Hodges, or whatever her name is.

Make your wife understand at the outset that you are going to flatter Myrtle because you want to win the golf match. If she is the understanding sort, she may even join in the game by buttering up to Big Charley. However, a word of caution here. You don't want the gals to engage in a hair-pulling match on the thirteenth tee. Make sure Sylvia bats her eyes in such a way that Charley's wife won't see her.

I repeat, the main idea is to take your opponents' minds off golf, to the detriment of their game. And with those curvaceous creatures known as women around, this can be done quite easily.

Unless Big Charley is the jealous type, you can even offer to help his wife or girlfriend with her swing. This will necessitate your standing behind her and putting your arms about her, to guide her grip on the club. It will maybe make her think you are contemplating a play for her.

It may also make Big Charley think about you, too, which is all right if it disturbs his game, but not when it gets to the point of his thinking of wrapping a steel-shafted club about your neck. You have to play it by feel, here.

You must caution your wife against any such tricks by Big Charley. I wouldn't want to be the cause of a divorce in the family. But properly done, this bit of byplay is almost guaranteed to hurt the other fellow's game, even if it won't improve your own.

Girls are talkative creatures, in case you don't already know, so get Sylvia to yakk it up on the green when the other side is about to putt. A male golfer will overlook such a breach of etiquette on the part of a woman not his wife. He will seethe inside and maybe ask for silence, but he won't get to the point of apoplexy, the way he would if you had just spoken.

Tell Sylvia beforehand that it might be a great idea for her to talk fashions to Myrtle from time to time, so that Myrtle will be thinking about the new mink coat you have promised her (makes no difference if you have or not, except maybe to Sylvia). Myrtle will believe her and will start getting so mad at Big Charley, who is stingy with a buck when it comes to Myrtle's clothes, that she may even deliberately begin to waste strokes.

This will get Big Charley mad, in turn. And his game will go out the window.

Most men will trudge down the fairways in more or less complete silence. Their minds for the most part are intent on their next shots. But the women—bless them—think of a thousand and one other things besides the little white ball and what they are going to hit it with when they finally reach it. It is at times like this that Sylvia can mention the mink coat or the cute little nightie or the stunning new dress that will put Myrtle into a tailspin.

Some wives will not play this game. So you have to lie a little, even before you get to the first tee. "Honey, how'd you like that silver-fox jacket you've been talking about? If we have a good day today and beat the Smiths, I may be able to pick it up for you."

You will then explain that beating the Smiths means more than money to you. Your wife will have that silver-fox jacket in her eyes while she listens to your game plan. She may even agree to mention the jacket to Myrtle, but *not* the fact that it is obtainable only by beating her and Charley.

Winning this game must mean something to you, however.

You can't go around buying furs or whatever for your wife every time you go out to play golf. Golf costs enough all by itself, so save this one for a very special occasion.

There is also reverse psychology to be mentioned here. You are going to play at golf-downmanship. You are playing a very important client and his wife. You want your client to win. So you must coach your wife a little differently.

Assuming your darling is a very good player, and Mary and John Walker, your client and his wife, are duffers, you must get your wife to agree to throw the game. This may not be easy. Good golfers look on any such jiggery-pokery with jaundiced eyes.

But if the loss of the game may mean a big contract,

then you hit your wife with the offer of the silver fox. If it is a very large contract, indeed, you may even go so far as to promise her that new car she wants. This all depends on individual circumstance and must be carefully thought out before the first word is spoken.

The same rule goes for your boss, though not on such a grand scale. You could probably get your frau's assistance by buying her a new dress or even a hat. The boss, or the client, must win at all costs, even if it shrinks your pocketbook momentarily. You can always make up the difference with a big contract or a nice raise.

You cannot be too obvious about these matters. You and your wife must appear to be playing to the best of your ability. However, this is where that good-luck charm comes in. You leave it home, and you mention this fact to the boss, so that he will think you are out to beat him, at least.

Now, there are many bosses who like to bend an elbow during the golf game. For this purpose they will carry with them small flasks, usually of sterling silver if they are very well-to-do bosses, and will pause from time to time to sample their contents.

You will be offered the flask. This is an important moment. A chill wind is blowing, and you happen to enjoy a nip of the sauce, which will warm you up. It is all very tempting. Willpower counts highly here. You accept the flask with a big grin, say thanks, and put it to your lips—and your tongue to the opening. This last bit is most important. Be sure the tongue fits closely.

Never cheat at a time like this. Your job may depend on it. You need a clear head, because you have a tough row to hoe ahead of you.

Only when the flask is firmly stoppered by your tongue do you tilt your head back and pretend to have a sip. You do not swallow any of the Canadian Club or the Napoleon brandy or the twenty-five-year-old Ambassador scotch that your boss can afford. Not a drop.

However, you pretend to do so.

You take the flask from your lips with a long-drawn sigh of approval and hand it back. Now you have an excuse to make a lousy shot or two. If your boss can drink you under the table, this is all to the good. He will be thinking he has put one over on you, and this is just as it should be, since he is your boss.

Maybe you even say that you never drink on the job, but this is a fun time, and so you pretend to have another swig when he offers it. He will chortle to himself, or maybe out loud, because he is the guy who pays your salary or sees to it that the organization pays it, which is much the same thing.

You realize what you are doing, don't you? You are flattering the boss, in a very subtle way. You are letting him think he is doing you one in the eye, which makes him think he is a very smart fellow. You must never let him realize that you are not actually drinking.

If you have a boss who is not drinking but only pretending to, this poses a problem. If neither of you is actually drinking, the boss, when he goes home or maybe even before, will find that the liquor in his flask is not diminishing, and this could be very embarrassing.

So you must watch him closely. If you believe that he is not drinking, then you're going to have to. I see no other way out of this dilemma except to go whole hog and really let the stuff trickle down your throat. Your boss has beaten you at the game.

But because he is the boss, you may be doing yourself a favor by getting sloshed. You will lose the game to him, which you intended doing anyhow, and you will have been made the patsy for his small bit of skullduggery. I approve of this only when the boss is not drinking himself.

Weigh the flask gently with your hand when he hands it to you. If it feels perceptibly lighter, you know at once that he is downing the sauce. If the flask weighs just as much as when he first drew it out, I'm afraid there's nothing to do but swallow.

I must mention one facet of this particular bit of golf-upmanship. Never let your fuddled state permit you to play better because you are feeling the drinks. This is very bad form. Some men I know play far better golf when they are three sheets to the wind than they do when they are stone-cold sober. It serves to relax them. If liquor affects you in this way, all you can do is resort to your willpower.

You must conquer yourself, and by this I mean you must force yourself to make poor shots. This takes a lot out of you, I know. But it's better to do that than to beat your boss and have him glowering at you all week long and wondering if it might not be better to eliminate your job and you at the same time.

I mention this drinking bit because golf is basically a sociable game. When men hit a little white ball on the green grass and sniff the fresh air, it parches their throats and gives them a thirst that cannot be quenched in any other way than by bellying up to the bar at the clubhouse after the game. Liquor loosens tongues and adds a piquant flavor to a game that has been adjudged by certain critics to be that of lunatics. It makes everybody feel he is a jolly good fellow. You may even feel this way yourself about the man who has just beaten you so badly.

Tomorrow will be another day. Or so the bottom of your glass will say.

While on the subject of drinking, another good ploy to use, particularly if you're involved in an important match you are really anxious to win, is to suggest stopping for a drink and a bite of lunch after the first nine holes. The thing to do is to urge your opponent to have a couple of martinis while you stick to beer. If he's just thirsty and not hungry, all the better. Two martinis on a fairly empty stomach can often produce some interesting results on a golf course. Your opponent may begin to see two or three balls instead of one when he's ready to take a poke at his next tee shot.

If the guy isn't a drinker, then urge some food on him—maybe a couple of big hamburgers with onions and tomatoes—anything to make him feel stuffed and loggy afterward (while you just order a hot dog or a lean corned beef on rye and only eat half of the sandwich), so that he begins to lose his competitive edge.

No other game I know seems to call for a nip every other hole or even more often. A tennis player will fall flat on his face if asked to hit swiftly moving tennis balls when he is drinking at the end of every game. But a golfer can walk and stand up and perhaps even manage to hit the ball when a large amount of scotch, rye, brandy, or gin nestles warmly in his middle.

Of course, if the boss is downing those shots regularly as he steps off the greens after his final putt, you have nothing to worry about. Sober, you can take an extra putt or two, or hook a drive when occasion demands it, so that the boss will win. Or a very important client, which amounts to much the same thing.

You will be blind to his cheating, too.

If he says he got a six on a hole when you know damn well he took an eight, you will make yourself smile and congratulate him. This is very important. Your boss—or client—must be made to feel that he is king of the hill. Man, your very living, and maybe your new set of wheels, depends on it.

I have never been able to figure out why golf practically forces a man to lie so much. I guess it's because a lot of us play it in the rough where nobody is around to count our strokes. Three becomes two or even one, at times when we know we are safe from discovery.

Vanity. That must be it. Nobody wants to be thought a complete duffer. One always wants to make a good showing in front of his fellowman. And so your golfer will lie and cheat—after all, it's just a stroke or two, so what does it matter?—as he wends his way from tee to rough and sand trap and that patch of sumac behind the green.

If you have a playing partner who walks with you to the lie of your ball and stands there as you swing, you must be very circumspect in your stroke counting. This is a very definite must. You must never, ever, be caught subtracting from your stroke total, or you will get a very bad name among your golfing buddies. And we just can't have that!

Subtlety is the first rule you must memorize.

Only when you are positive that you are safe from observation do you nudge the ball with your foot, moving it to a better lie. This is extremely difficult on the fairways when you are out in full view of everybody, unless, of course, you are playing winter rules, which permit you to improve your lie in the fairway by nudging the ball with the clubhead. It becomes downright impossible on the greens.

The rough affords you the best chance of all. Here you may be hidden by trees or underbrush and can kick the ball with a toe without its being noticed. You really need only a few of these to better your otherwise honest score.

I mention all these tidbits because I am talking about playing golf with other people. Naturally, if you go around alone, you can cheat to your heart's content. Only you will ever know.

But never brag about the 75 you scored when you were playing alone, because the handicapper may hear about it, and if you boast about enough of these rounds, your handicap will be lowered. This is very bad, indeed, in certain cases.

Furthermore, your golf friends will want to play around with you, and if you begin to shoot over 100 time and again where there are witnesses to see it, your 75 scorecard will become extremely suspect.

Brag if you must. But do it with other friends, friends who do not play golf and don't know any golfers who know you. If you can find such friends, that is. Otherwise, you must keep your mouth shut. There just isn't any way out of this bind.

I have certain golf buddies who keep two score-cards. One they show publicly to their acquaintances. The other, which records their true score, they are wont to stare at very disconsolately in the privacy of their own kitchens, late at night and with a fifth martini in their grubby little paws.

Oh, you can cheat a little, and it may not affect your handicap or your relations with your golf pals. If you normally card 100, and you bring in a score of 95, nobody is going to faint dead away. It may even earn you a few words of praise and an encouraging clap on the shoulder. What you have done here is ignore only five strokes.

There was that whiff on the second fairway when you took your eye off the ball and that extra stroke in the sand trap on the third. They weren't so bad, were they? Of course not. You can hardly even remember them. You talk to yourself like this, and pretty soon you have forgotten them, even in your subconscious.

Now you consider the ball you knocked into the water at the eleventh. You replaced your ball, but you didn't count a stroke, which you should have. Big deal, you sneer. And then there were the two strokes you took in the rough, only one of which you marked down. So what? It was the second shot you hit out of the rough that really counted, because it was a beauty. Ignore the first one.

And that stupid shank you hit when two-ironing your way toward the seventeenth green was just one of those practice shots you take from time to time. It shouldn't be counted against you that the ball got in the way of your club, should it? Certainly not!

Five little mistakes. Easy to dismiss from your mind; easy to say they don't matter. But they make a difference in your score.

So you just ignore those mistakes, nor does your conscience bother you. It is a mental game we golfers play, something like self-hypnosis. In my opinion we do this because golf is a game you play by yourself, no matter how many partners you have going around the course with you. It is so easy to lie and cheat a little. Why? Because you are lying to yourself.

And that is very different from lying to your fellowman, though this is also involved, eventually. You will find that you will be having a mild conversation with yourself, like so:

"I scored a five on this par-four hole," you mutter to yourself.

Your conscience digs you with, "Now wait a minute. There was that stroke in the rough, following which you hit that great seven-iron shot onto the lip of the green. You haven't marked it down."

"Ah, who's to know? Charley didn't see it."

"You saw it!"

"Yes, but I'm the one who says it doesn't count."

You write down a five.

This harms nobody, really, if you aren't playing for money. Every man alive has lied to himself at one time or another. So you lie to yourself at golf.

You aren't walking up to Charley and telling him you scored a five. You just mark it down on the score-card that you are keeping for your own amusement. Of course, Charley will ask you what you shot, and you will show him your scorecard.

What this means is: This is the way you *think* you shot that hole. It's the way you play, in other words. If Charley doesn't care for the way you score your own game, that's his tough luck, unless Charley actually saw you take that extra shot in the rough, which you haven't put down. This will make a difference. There are some sticklers who will enumerate out loud the number of shots you took, telling you about each one in detail. Shun such spoilsports.

By and large, however, you will be off by yourself in the rough when you make the flub. Charley will be walking toward his own ball, or ought to be. It is always best to cheat when you know that Charley is off in another corner of the rough, having his own problems. The guy can't be watching you and hunting for his own ball at the same time, can he?

On putting greens, however, it is difficult to cheat.

First, because everybody is staring right at you. The ball is right there, a round white pellet on green grass, and everyone can see you miss those three putts because the sun is shining and they all have twenty-twenty vision. So you admit your mistakes at putting. What the hell else can you do?

Still, sometimes you can concede putts to yourself (if your opponents will let you get away with it). Say, a putt of from four inches inward to the cup. Every golf player makes those easy ones, doesn't he? No, but you ignore this. You pick your ball up with an air of saying a putt like that is beneath your dignity. Or you casually one-hand the putt toward the cup indicating your opinion that it's an automatic "gimme." Even if the ball missed, your careless one-handed poke shows your opponent you figure he conceded the shot anyway.

If your fellow players scream about it, as they have been known to do, you must putt. There's no way out of that one. None.

A note about golf etiquette when on the greens: If your ball is lying in the path of another ball, you courteously lift it off the green and mark its position with a flat marker.

This marker can be individualized with your initials; it can be gold or sterling silver or just plain chrome. The idea is that the fellow farthest from the hole putts first and your ball may lie between his ball and the hole, thus constituting a hazard that may be removed.

Sometimes you can conveniently forget the position of your ball and drop the ball a little closer to the cup as you lift your marker to take your own putt, all in one deft movement. This may or may not help, because you really can't drop your ball so far from its original lie that nobody will notice. All these little details must be performed with extreme subtlety.

Of course, you can always kick your ball closer to the cup, pretending to stumble, but I don't recommend this to be done more than once in any eighteen holes. Golfers have been shot for less. It helps if you have been drinking, for then you'll have some sort of excuse. Otherwise, you have none at all.

Always remember, whether you are playing a two-ball or a four-ball game, that your opponents are reasonably intelligent people. Never insult that intelligence. They will resent it, and you, too.

Better to lose the game than have that happen!

7

How the Game Is Really Played: The Pros

The professionals of the game of golf, those men whom you and I hold most in awe, play very much by the rules of golf. There can be no fooling around where they are concerned. Because these men and women play a very grim game, they have judges to whom they can appeal and a golf association that can bar an individual from play when one breaks those rules as a matter of habit.

What we have been speaking about so far, we have been discussing with tongue in cheek. There is no such expression when Julius Boros tees off in a match with Arnold Palmer.

To such men, golf is a way of life. It is big business. Where fifty thousand dollars may be riding on a game, you watch your strokes carefully, and you don't cheat. There is always an audience if you are a big name. The pin becomes the flagstick, the sand trap a bunker, and the four-ball match is not a foursome. There are rules for almost any circumstance that may arise during a match.

Know your golf rules if you are a really serious golfer. These rules are distributed in little booklets anywhere you buy your golf clubs or other equipment. They are free for the asking. Own one.

Such rules are memorized and long forgotten by the great ones. They know them almost instinctively, as a football player knows that an incomplete forward pass stops the clock. For those of you who may be thinking of a career in golf, my advice is to study them.

Once you have mastered your game, and these rules, the game of golf offers entrancing rewards for its superior players. Most of them will be the pros at various golf courses. This means they are hired professional golf players for these particular country clubs and will be paid salaries. They will also make money from maintaining pro shops in which you can buy sweaters endorsed by Arnie Palmer, socks on which Lee Trevino may have stamped his approval, shoes of the sort worn by Jack Nicklaus, to say nothing of a Gary Player putter or a Doug Sanders two-iron.

The golf pro will give you lessons at a moderate or costly figure, depending on the status of your golf club. No matter what you pay, if you benefit by these, they are worth the cost. The trouble is that most people

take these lessons, then also accept advice from their friends. Do only what the pro tells you, even if you have to dig into your wallet for another buck or two to take some more lessons. It's worth it in the long run.

You have already seen that the golf pro will be able to make himself a very comfortable living. This is only right and proper.

Let us say that this particular pro is one of the supergolfers. He will normally lend his name to the club, but will rarely be on duty. He will be off on the golf circuits to add to his income. Who can blame him? The prizes they give these days at golf tournaments would tempt old Croesus himself.

It doesn't stop there. Let us assume that our golf pro has won the Masters and the British Open. This makes his name very much a household word, indeed. It also opens up very lucrative doors.

He will be asked to write a book, perhaps. Gary Player, Tommy Armour, and Patty Berg are some great golfers who have published books on the game. There are many others, so many that when you go to buy a book on golf, your head will reel at the offerings.

Our golf pro may be asked to write a column on golf for a newspaper syndicate. These little columns are usually illustrated with a couple of line drawings of a golfer doing his thing. I have read such advisory columns by Arnie Palmer, Cary Middlecoff, and Jack Nicklaus. There are others.

Money begins accumulating in really big amounts. None of your $35,000-a-year golf pro jobs here. The big names in golf make big money, and don't you ever forget it.

But don't be jealous.

Just as you pay a doctor for all the years he went to premed and then medical school, for his years of internship and the knowledge he has acquired over those years, so these super-golf stars are reaping the rewards of unending hours of sweat and toil, mastering the game that is their life.

When we hear of Ben Hogan, we never remember those hours when his hands became bloody and blistery while making golf shots over and over, nor of how he would tape his hands and go on practicing until the blood came seeping through those bandages, to learn one particular pitch shot. His fellow pros regarded him as a machine because of his tremendous dedication to achieving perfection.

Another man who made himself into what seemed an automaton that never made mistakes was Bobby Jones. He was a very young man when he won his first tournament, as was Gene Sarazen. They had practiced and practiced during their boyhood years, almost as though they were fulfilling a fate mapped out for them on the Norns' looms.

Such as you and I may not have this calling. We're weekend golfers, and we enjoy the game—more or less—while we marvel at the accomplishments of the Trevinos, the Palmers, the Players. We tend to forget that these men were not born with a golf club in their hands. They learned this trade they are following, even as you and I learned our own particular trades.

It is only in recent years, of course, that the golf pro has been something of a sports idol, like a Tom Seaver or a Joe Namath. In those early times when golf was first beginning to grow, the professional golfer was rather looked down upon as a lesser breed—something the way actors and actresses used to be regarded in the early years of the nineteenth century. All this has changed, as well we know.

I suppose the best example of this adulation of great golfers is Arnie Palmer. Everybody has heard of Arnie's army that traipses around the course with him, oohing and ahing at his marvelous shots and even groaning when—yes!—even Arnold Palmer fails to quite achieve that miraculous shot that will bring him on the green in two, but lands him in the bunker instead.

The result of this adulation has put money into Arnie's wallet. I have it on good authority that it will cost ten thousand dollars to have him lecture your social group on golf. Before he became a corporation, he would be offered only five hundred. Today, he has some of the most prestigious business firms in the United States paying him fees for endorsements and such, including the designing of new golf courses.

Jack Nicklaus is another superstar who is making it big in the world of finance because of his golfing abilities. At one time, I am given to understand, he used the same money-management corporation that handles Arnie, but now he is out on his own. He also will buy up golf clubs and courses, as does Palmer, lending them the glamour of his name.

These men are sitting pretty today because they can

do things with woods and irons and putters that few other men can do. Such things as the hundred-plus sand traps (bunkers) at the Oakland Country Club do not bother them nearly as much as they would you or me. They have practiced until they have mastered the strokes that will bring them over or past those hazards.

Jack Nicklaus, for instance, taught himself to play golf left-handed in order to play those lies that are all but impossible for a right-handed player. When the ball comes to rest an inch away from a stone wall or a tree, nobody on earth is going to be able to attack that ball from a right-handed stance. So Jack, aware that shots like this will crop up in the game, even as the pros play it, taught himself to hit that ball by swinging lefty.

Not an easy feat. But this is why Jack Nicklaus will command big fees in his appearances.

No, Jack doesn't carry left-handed and right-handed clubs in his golf bag. What he does is this: Taking a regular club, he uses it left-handed in such a manner that the grip is reversed and he hits the ball with the face of the club pointing downward, the narrow end touching the ground and the ball as he swings.

In his book on golf Gary Player describes just such a situation. His lie was at the base of a stone wall. Instead of tackling the ball left-handed, as Jack Nicklaus might have done, Gary decided to try a ricochet shot. He hit it perfectly—but then it came right back and hit him perfectly, knocking him out.

When he recovered, he used a chip shot to get onto

the green and holed out, confident that he had tied for the lead. Then came the real blow. He was informed that because the ball had hit him in flight, he was being penalized for interfering with the ball! Maybe those golf pros don't have it so easy, after all!

The big enemy of the great golfers is their nerves, as Tommy Armour has pointed out. In one of the books on golf that he has written he speaks of the "yips"— that particular bit of screaming nerves that occurs to a superstar when he bends over to make a short putt. Even the immortal Bobby Jones was subject to them. The cause is tension.

When you are playing for stakes of fifty thousand dollars, more or less, and you are right up there with the leaders, there develops inside you a little demon that runs along your nerve ends and makes your hands shake, makes you concentrate on anything but the golf ball and the putt you need to sink it.

Armour points out that the yips involve only short golf putts; they have nothing to do with wood and iron play. Indeed, almost all the nerves of the super-golfers seem to shred on the putting green. When they have been in the golf wars a long time, their wood and iron shots are almost perfect; it is on the greens with a fortune often riding on a simple putt that their nerves sometimes rebel.

It is this nervous strain that made Ben Hogan and Tommy Armour himself give up tournament golf. So it isn't all peaches and cream with the pros. They are human beings like you and me, though it isn't a bout of the yips or nerves that ruins our game; it's just inept, inaccurate play.

It's the fact that we forget to keep our left arms straight when using woods and irons, or fail to keep our eye on the spot where the ball was, just before we stroked it gently with the putter, that ruins our scores. The pros don't do these things, because playing a shot accurately is a matter of habit with them. It's the nerves of their human bodies that sometimes gets to them, after a while, due to the constant strain of playing for big money.

Consistency is the correct word to use in referring to the pros. They know the course they are scheduled to play, or they make it their business to familiarize themselves with it before they step onto the first tee in the tournament being held there. All greens are different, far more so than the fairways or the roughs, and it is to these greens that the great players will address their attentions.

They will play these greens in practice rounds, noting their rolls and slopes, the speed and grain of the grass. This information will be neatly stashed away in their memory banks when they come to play for money. Golf is a matter of business with them.

Most golfers play their home course until they know it as they recognize their wife's voice. The pros are always on the move. They will travel from the Pleasant Valley course in Massachusetts to the Oakmont in Pittsburgh, Pennsylvania, to the Oak Hill course in Rochester, New York, to the many and varied California and Florida courses. They may play on a different course every week or every other week. They must learn the vagaries of each course before playing over it for their livelihoods.

Of course, these men will make the great shots, those that are talked about in whispers at the nineteenth holes from the rocky shores of Maine to the cable-car lines of San Francisco. And just as the long bomb or a goal-line defense will often spur a football team on to victory, so a terrific shot will act as the stimulus to make a pro play slightly better than is his custom, to win a big one.

Such a great shot was the one made by British golfer Ted Ray at East Lake, a long time ago. His drive had put him on a line with a huge tree, just this side of which was a big mound. He could not shoot through the tree to put him on the green, and the tree was forty feet high. Yet Ray used a mashie niblick to lift his ball over the tree and plop it down on the green!

You have all seen your friends—or maybe you've done it yourself—execute a truly great shot. For once in your life, everything seemed to click. Zeppo Marx has said that his greatest shot was to hit a tree, have his ball bounce through a sand trap, and hit a stone to soar up on a ricochet to the green and into the cup. As a matter of fact, Zeppo adds, it was so difficult, it was the only time he ever made it.

I guess all of us have made shots like that, at one time or another, when Lady Luck was beaming upon us with special indulgence. I, too, have hit a tree with a sliced ball and watched it bound onto the fairway, leaving me with a perfect pitch shot onto the green. If only luck would smile on us a little more.

I am always discouraged by reading about how good the pros are, probably because I know I will never be able to match their figures. Ben Hogan averaged 69.30 for all the golf courses and all the games he played in the year 1948. This, to my knowledge, is the lowest golf-score average for a year of professional golf—or any other kind of golf, for that matter—on record.

Arnie Palmer averaged 69.86 one year.

Can you imagine an average like that, for a whole year's play? It's things like that that discourage me, where golf is concerned. I have even heard of a man who can kick a golf ball around the course and score a 70. Such information makes me want to throw my bag of clubs in the nearest water hazard, as other golfers have been known to do upon occasion.

If you really want to depress yourself, take a peek into the pages of the *Guinness Sports Record Book*. There you will note that the lowest score ever made on an eighteen-hole golf course with a par 70 or better is— hold your breath—only 55! Sounds absolutely impossible, doesn't it? There is also a record of a man scoring only 25 on a nine-hole course.

I don't know. Either the gods who bedevil golfers were staring off into space on that day or a brisk wind must have been blowing, straight from heaven itself.

I enjoy these record books. How long would you say it took to play the fastest round of golf? Yes, I mean eighteen holes.

Would you believe it was done in 14 minutes, 2.2

seconds? It takes me longer than that to walk from the tee on the first to its green!

How would you like to be able to drive your ball from the tee onto the green on a 483-yard hole? It happened in England. Okay, the wind was blowing, but even so. Craig Wood hit the longest drive ever recorded at a tournament in 1933. His ball traveled 430 yards. It happened in the Open Championship at the Old Course in St. Andrews, Scotland.

Then there is John Hudson, who shot two consecutive holes in one during a tournament at the Martini International course (how's that for the name of a golf course?) in Norwich, England. His first was scored with a four-iron on a par-three, 195-yard hole.

On the next hole, the twelfth, he slammed his drive up and over some trees between the tee and the green. His ball sailed majestically above all that foliage and sank out of sight. It was another one-shotter.

Unfortunately, Hudson didn't win the tournament. But he made sure his name would go down in the record books! That's a kind of instant fame, if you ask me.

A lot of this tournament golf isn't dramatic at all. Somebody—you name him: Nicklaus, Palmer, Trevino, or one of the other greats—gets out in front on the first round and stays there, hitting tee shots straight as arrows, using his irons the way Tommy Armour did, putting like the true master he is. No yips or tense nerves, at least on the surface.

But there are tournaments when the drama builds up and up, and away. Take the 1971 Masters, when

Jack Nicklaus felt he had it in his bag, all the way. Along comes Charlie Coody out of Texas and puts four marvelous rounds together to stop him. This cost Jack the Grand Slam. There are so many good golfers on the pro tours that almost any individual pro can get hot and string together four rounds of superb golf to walk off with the top prize money.

Usually, somebody like Nicklaus or Palmer will do that, but there are times when the comparatively little known men come through. Not that they aren't fine golfers, which they are, but they just don't get the publicity.

When they string enough of those big wins together, then they will get the publicity and go on to the big money. Which is what any man wants, when he is a pro golfer.

And yet—any golf professional will tell you that there are times when even his best shots do not work. Tommy Armour sliced tee shots out of bounds four times on the sixth hole at Merion, during the 1934 Open. In this same golf classic the great Gene Sarazen slammed two balls into the water hazard at the eleventh hole.

It was this same course, at the fifth hole, that is generally blamed for Jack Nicklaus not winning the 1971 Open, by driving his tee shot into the water. It is this same Jack Nicklaus who shares with Lee Trevino the record for going around Merion four times and carding a 273.

So you can see golf is sometimes an in-and-out game, even for the professionals, just as it is for you and me.

Then there is that part of the game of golf called tournament play. This need not concern you unless you are entered in your club tournament, or aspire to enter, to match your play with that of the club elite, or even against that of the men who make their living by playing golf.

Tournament golf is an entirely different breed of cat. It is the pros' way of life, to begin with, for they are almost always on the tournament trail, playing at Westchester one week, at Merion another, perhaps at Cypress Point on the third. For these professionals, the tournaments are where they make their living.

Some play in more tournaments than others. Some golf pros only enter a few. But the big names attend all the important ones; they must win first or second money at Pebble Beach or the Augusta National more often than not to be considered a good provider for the family.

Therein lies the rub. These men are playing golf for a living. They are kin to the doctors who are performing heart transplants, to the lawyers who are trying cases for General Motors. This game of golf is their livelihood. And naturally enough, they get uptight about it.

They become nervous, tense, even more so than you or I. The putt that may put a buck or two in our wallets will sometimes put fifty thousand (or more) in theirs. We all know how tough it is to sink a twenty- or a thirty-footer. Imagine Frank Beard or Billy Casper as they sight their ball and the hole, knowing so much money rides on whether or not they make the ball drop in that little cup.

No wonder they get the yips, or that tension frays nerves already shredded by a thousand other putts on a thousand other courses. The marvel to me is the fact that they can putt at all. My hands would be shaking so much, I couldn't even grip the putter.

Ah, yes. It's wonderful when the putt is made and the round is won, when his name goes up on the list as number one. It means that this golfer has mastered not only his clubs, the course, and his opponents, but also his nerves. He has fought the tenseness and the quivering of the muscles that spells the difference between a great shot and a poor one.

And he will need a certain number of those great shots to see his name, like that of Abou Ben Adam, lead all the rest. For any golfer will make mistakes. He is a human being. I am confident that both Jack Nicklaus and Arnie Palmer will testify to this, as well as hosts of other pros who have ever played the game for tournament stakes.

A man can fight nerves only so long. A moment of inattention, a single degree of lessened concentration, will cause the club to vary its angle, the ball to go where he does not want it. All great professionals know this and are constantly fighting to maintain that concentration, that impassivity that will allow them to do all the right things that will place them among the top money-winners.

Quite often, if he is married and has children, a golfer will bring his family with him on the tournament circuit. It must be hard, after having gone five or six over par, to come home to the little woman and all those trusting young faces and realize that the few mistakes you made will mean everybody has to tighten his belt and skimp so as to afford the gasoline to drive on to the next golf course.

These worries are constantly in a man's mind as he drives along the highways that will take him to his next test. He will agonize over a bad lie that cost two strokes, he may mentally damn the deer that came bounding onto the fairway at Cypress Point and caused him to take a four before he was even on the green.

Hope will sustain him. He will make his big killing at Indian Wells or Pensacola, he tells himself as the road unwinds under his wheels. He will not make the same mistake he made at Westchester. Yet in his heart he knows he will make other mistakes, ones he did not anticipate. Constantly, the professional golfer has to be on guard.

He hopes for a sunny day without too much wind. He hopes that the greenkeeper will have modified the slope on the fourteenth green that always gives him so much trouble. He hopes a thousand and one things.

All this hoping is just another word for worry.

He worries about his daughter who has a bad cold and whether it will turn into pneumonia. He must also, in a corner of his mind, worry about the fact that he may catch cold, which won't be so good when he gets to Torrey Pines and faces the dogleg at the tenth.

He will remember Ben Hogan and his car accident, he will recall the time Jack Cupit pulled a back muscle, or how Frank Beard developed encephalitis, yet recovered to go on and win tournament after tournament. There are others, but these will do for a real pro to worry about. And when he gets tired of that, there's always the errant golf ball that can hit you, as it did Doug Sanders, on the elbow yet.

There are twelve million men and women playing golf in the United States today. There are more than eight thousand golf courses. The pro must wonder about the new phenoms that will be coming along, as every veteran in every money sport must wonder. In some sports the newcomer will take away the veteran's job. In golf it amounts almost to the same thing. The newcomer may beat him out of money needed to support his family.

It can be a very trying game, this golf.

There have been men who have appeared on the horizon, who have flashed brilliantly for a little while and then faded.

Where did they go?

Well, a lot of them just could not face the stiff competition day after day, week after week, throughout the year. They have nerves, as have all human beings, and their nerves tightened up too much, after such a steady pounding. They realized it was not worth the beating they were taking, physically and mentally. Far better to retire to their home course where they have a job as a golf pro, can make a good living, and enjoy life a little.

The pressure is just too great.

Nobody wins forever. There are always losers. And

among the losers, in various tournaments, you will find some very big names, indeed. Nobody is always on his game. There are a thousand factors to be considered —health, wind, the type of course, the other guy who is making a fantastic score while playing like some kind of machine, mental attitude, degree of worry, financial status. What worries us, worries a pro.

Some golfers like certain courses better than others. If he is a long-ball hitter, he likes the long courses, where his 300-yard drives will give him an advantage. A good putter will like the tough greens, where his skill will reduce his score while adding strokes to those of his competitors.

The strange course is anathema to the professional. If he has never teed off on the Mauna Kea Beach Hotel course, which has hosted tournaments, he will approach its greens and fairways with some anxiety. He will have to practice on it, and sometimes even a professional does not get much of a chance to practice. For Mauna Kea, you can read any other golf course that the pro has never seen.

He has little time to become accustomed to the vagaries of a course. The tournament usually lasts four days, during which time he is out playing golf for money. Then when it ends, he pushes his clubs into his bag into his car or trailer and goes on to a completely different course.

Remember, all this time he is playing for a living.

They even have machines now that add to his problem. Mowers for golf greens used to cut a twenty-two-inch swath. Now they have more up-to-date equipment that cuts a swath of more than fifty inches. This means that the grass will be smoother over a wider area. It also means that the pro will have to take note of this and compensate for it.

While we're on the subject of greens, how'd you like to hole a 163-foot putt? You can, if you're both good and lucky, on the eleventh green at Bellerive in Missouri. The sixth hole will let you sink one of 120 feet, ditto the luck.

Some courses earn nicknames. Ben Hogan called the Oakland Hills course in a Detroit suburb the "green monster." Usually, however, as I've already mentioned, it's the individual holes that are given special names by the pros.

Naturally, I can't write down what some of them call certain holes. I keep thinking of the seventh at Pebble Beach, said to be the most photographed golf hole in the world, where you have to drive at a green beyond which lies the Pacific Ocean, with sand traps and some rough in between. Another such is the sixth at Sun Valley, where you must shoot over some trees and a stream of water that bisect the so-called fairway, to get a chance to putt. They call the eighteenth hole at Pebble Beach "The Finisher." As it is, again and again.

No, the life of the golf pro is not all peaches and whipped cream, despite the mental image you have formed. What amazes me is that more of them don't develop ulcers.

So when you're going around in anywhere from 80 to 140, just reflect on one thing. You don't have to play this game for a living.

So be glad.

8

***

Let's Play Around Together

Having read this far, you are now ready for your golf test. We are going to assume that you and your wife are going to play against Big Charley and his wife, Myrtle. For the nonce, your wife is named Sylvia. And for wife, as I have said before, you can read girlfriend.

This match is very important to you. Big Charley has been spreading the word that he and his wife, Myrtle, can take any other player and his wife who are members of the country club, excluding only the golf pro. Now, you play a good game, you shoot in the low 80's most of the time, and every once in a while you manage to get into the high 70's.

Sylvia and Myrtle play about even, in the low 90's. You figure that if Sylvia can hold Myrtle even, the match will depend on how well you and Charley play. Big Charley is a braggart and a windbag. You know the type. His drives are the best ever made, his iron shots are the equal of Tommy Armour's (he should be so good), and his putts drop in like those of Arnie Palmer. According to Charley, that is.

The guy is good, you admit that, but he isn't as good as he says he is (nobody could be). And last Saturday night at the club dance, when you were more than somewhat in your cups, you issued a challenge to him. He was also deep in the sauce, but he will remember the challenge, and next day he will call you up to learn if you really meant what you said about playing him and Myrtle for ten bucks a hole and a century note on the entire eighteen.

You can't possibly back out. Not to Charley. He'd spread the word the way your oldest child spreads strawberry jam on bread and butter. Of course you meant the challenge, you will say. Certainly you intend to bet a sawbuck a hole and have another hundred riding on the match. Chicken feed, you hint, but it will sweeten up the game. Inwardly, you may be dying, but you must never let this be known.

At worst, you stand to lose $280, plus the fact that you will have to listen to Big Charley telling the golf world how he and Myrtle took you and Sylvia over the course jumps.

Times like this happen to all of us every once in a while. In tennis, in golf, in Ping-Pong, or even, I guess, in chess. Your male ego rises in total wrath at the braggadocio of a fellow player, and you put your foot

in your mouth. So what else is new? Could matters get much worse?

Indeed, they could. You now have to tell Sylvia about the challenge and the bet. You must tell her. After all, she is one of the four-ball group. And she will hit the ceiling as she has only rarely been known to do in all the otherwise happy years of your marriage.

"Two hundred and eighty dollars? On a golf game?" she screams so the people in the next town can hear her. "Are you out of your skull completely?"

You are, you admit, but this is where you must apply some of that golf psychology I've been rapping about. This is a prelim psych bit, if you want a name for it.

You say to her, lying through your teeth, "Charley said his Myrtle could give you aces and spades and still beat you five up and four to go."

Sylvia pauses and gets a funny look in her eyes. Now, it's a queer thing, but women don't often feel the same way about golf as do men. Yet the idea of Big Charley saying his wife can beat her all hollow stirs up Sylvia's female hormones.

"He did, did he?" she mutters.

Charley never said anything of the kind, but you aren't going to admit that to Syl, are you? Damn right, you're not. So you have to begin lying long before you set your cleats on the fairway. That is, if you want your wife to live amicably with you.

"I couldn't let him get away with that," you add.

You will notice how adroitly you have sidestepped her question. You haven't exactly lied here; you've merely diverted her interest. It might even help if you say in a gruffly tender voice, "Nobody can say that about my wife!"

This will make her think you're a loyal husband and maybe you still do love her, after all. Such tactics are always good.

She should say, right about here and perhaps a little worriedly, "Do you think we can take them?" She is just about hooked, but you still have to play her a little more.

"I've been wanting to buy you that new pin you admired so much at [the local jeweler], the thing with the tiny emeralds in it. You said it was three hundred bucks. If we can win the match and maybe a few holes —by God, I'll buy it for you."

The hook sinks deep, but since she is your wife and naturally suspicious of such largess, she asks, "Do you really mean that, honey?"

"No matter how much I have to add to it," you declare gallantly.

So you may have to lay out an extra fifty iron men, always assuming you win the match and those holes. Isn't it worth that much to be able to crow over Big Charley? Besides, you'll be impressing Sylvia. And that's worth almost any amount of money.

You now have a real helpmate. Funny thing about women, if you can get them to ally themselves with you, their fertile brains can come up with some real good ideas. She hunches forward and with a hungry gleam in her green eyes that will match those emeralds of which she's thinking, she will be ready for your psychological game.

You tell her what you plan to do.

She evinces no shock, half the time. Women will sometimes reveal a very mercenary character when it comes to cheating at games being played for money. On the other hand, she may be dubious about some of it, all depending on what sort of girl she is. Usually, the gold pin is the clincher. Few women can resist a prize like that.

You both go to bed early every night for the rest of the week. You abstain from sex, like soldiers going into battle or athletes scheduled to perform on an Olympic field. You both become very dedicated human beings. You will go over in your mind the helpful hints I have already given you and plan on how to put them to the best use.

Dawns the big day, bright and sunny, with little wind. Sylvia dons the golf skirt she has made from a mini into a micro, to show off her good legs. She also wears a tight blouse. You put on that shirt of many colors, which you told Sylvia you wouldn't be seen dead in when her mother gave it to you.

Properly arrayed for combat, you drive to the country club. Big Charley shows up with Myrtle, and both of them blink a little when they see how you are arrayed, better than any lily of the field. Charley can't take his eyes off Sylvia's legs. Myrtle glares daggers at Charley.

Sylvia drives off first, waggling her posterior at Charley. Charley notices it, and Myrtle notices Charley.

Sylvia gets off a fine drive; Myrtle doesn't. You drive two hundred yards up the fairway, to a fine lie. Charley drives twenty yards beyond you.

So you put more of your psychological know-how to work and do the unexpected. You say, "That was a real beauty, Charley. I wish I had your power. You really put the wood to a ball."

Since you have already clued in Sylvia about these tactics, she smiles happily as she strides along with you and the others. She now bats her eyes at Charley and adds her own compliments to yours. This will make Charley feel great, but it will not do the same for his wife. She will see your wife making eyes at her husband, and she will begin doing a slow burn. (See Chapter 6.)

Okay. You all get onto the green in easy stages. Myrtle is one down to Sylvia because she is getting mad. All you have to do at this point is play Charley even. So here you drag out that putter I told you about and with which you have been practicing more or less secretly. You kiss the shaft at this point, but you don't say anything.

If you don't have an old putter, remember the lucky piece. You will have invented one by this time, won't you? Or you can rub your wife's left elbow, telling everybody that this gives you a certain touch on the greens. This last bit has a twofold purpose. Not only will it psych Charley when and if you sink that long putt, it will make Myrtle even madder that Charley doesn't depend on her the way you do on Sylvia.

You win this hole by at least two strokes.

On the second tee, recalling what I have already said, you will stand where Charley cannot fail to see that wild shirt out of the corners of his eyes as he prepares to drive. If he asks you to stand back, as he will probably do, you agree and apologize. He may not ask you on this tee, but he certainly will on a subsequent one. You can bet on that.

It is very hard to cheat outright in a match like this, because your opponents will be watching you with eyes that can put those of an eagle to shame. You must not kick your ball to a better lie in the rough or bump it along with your club. You just have to play it straight, right about here.

But be of good cheer. For it is while you all walk down the fairway to the second green that Sylvia casually tells Myrtle that you insist on giving her that gold pin with the emeralds. No need to say they are only emerald chips. Let Myrtle really burn.

Sylvia must explain that you are giving it to her because you have finally come to your senses and realize how much work she does with your kids, how deftly she manages the budget, and how much fun she is to be with. Sylvia must never hint that the pin is a reward for winning at golf.

If she is anything like the female golfers I know, Myrtle's play will become erratic, to say the least, on this second hole. Her mind will be so filled with that pin, with how much you adore and appreciate Sylvia and how little attention her Charley pays to her, that her game ought to crumble like a sand castle at high tide.

Properly done, this should give you the game right then and there. Even if Charley plays like the superbeing he thinks he is, your Sylvia should outscore his Myrtle by so much that you will have $280 toward that gold pin without any more ado.

A word of advice. Always buy your wife the pin. Without fail, and even if you lose. You never know when some other guy who very much resembles Big Charley will start bragging and you will be in your cups again and issue that challenge. You want your wife to join in your game, because without her help, you can't win it.

Right about here I want to mention playing golf with priests, rabbis, and ministers. Chances are, your wife won't be along at such times, since these are usually stag affairs, so you're on your own.

These clerics have what I consider an unfair advantage in a way, or maybe they're only trying to psych *you*. I've never quite had the courage to ask the Reverend MacIntosh if he is praying as he addresses his ball or merely trying in his genteel way to do me one in the eye.

I see his lips move, I see his closed eyes, and I begin to wonder. Does God play golf? Does God lend a helping hand to those who serve Him? I have seen the Reverend MacIntosh pull off some almost miraculous shots every once in a while when he seems to have been praying, shots I would not ordinarily believe to be possible.

In such situations I always fall back on religion, too. Not that I pray. What are my prayers compared to those of a minister, a rabbi, or a priest? No, I merely sidle up to him as we walk along the fairway and ask rather confidentially, "Could you give me a little spiritual guidance, Father?" Or Reverend or Rabbi, as the case may be. "I've always been confused by the doctrine of transubstantiation."

Or whatever doctrine it is that may or may not confuse you. You will have to do your own research, here. It always helps if you know vaguely what you are talking about, or sound as if you do. You must never make the cleric suspicious of your intentions.

You will now have given him something to think about other than his golf game. He will scent a lost soul and strive to the best of his abilities to rescue you from hellfire. It never fails, this bit. No cleric worth his salt will fail to charge in with amens sounding at the prospect of winning a convert or bringing a laggard back to the church or the synagogue. It is his breath of life, his reason for being what he is.

Keep the discussion going as you wend your paths across the fairways. This is where golf has a decided advantage over a more active game such as tennis. It's very difficult indeed to conduct a theological argument while batting swiftly moving tennis balls. But golf! Ah! The sun shines, a balmy breeze blows, it is good to be alive and in that mood that permits men to indulge in an intellectual debate.

Never become so involved in this discussion that you forget your own game. This is a no-no. Just go on mumbling enough words to keep the cleric thinking and talking, trying ever harder to come upon an argument that will make him believe that he has won you over and snatched you back from eternal damnation.

Nine times out of ten, you will win the golf game.

If this rabbi, priest, or minister is a good friend, it will be well at the conclusion of the game to clasp his hand and declare fervently that he has made you see the light. This will take his mind off the fact that you have beaten him at golf. In his eyes the main point will be that he has saved your soul. Always concede this. What difference does it make to you what he thinks about your soul, now really?

You are thus preparing the way for another friendly game by keeping him in a good mood. During the days or weeks between games, you must do a bit of research and come up with another puzzling bit of theology that defies your powers of understanding. Don't make it too simple, though.

I have a number of good ones on the tip of my tongue when I set out to play golf with a cleric. This happens more often than you might think. There is always a member of the club who knows an astounding number of the religious. I know a few myself and enjoy their company, but some of these club members are downright holy.

A word of caution, here. You will find it very difficult to recognize a priest, say, on the links. It's fifty to one he looks more disreputable than you in his golfing attire, or if you are the clotheshorse type, he may outdo you in his sartorial splendor. Don't expect the Roman collar or funereally black garb. Far from it!

I mention this because you may find yourself playing

alongside Joe without realizing he is Monsignor Joseph J. O'Houlihan of the local parish. Or maybe Bishop Jeremiah Wilson of the Protestant group, or Rabbi Jacob Meyers from the synagogue on Main Street.

When in doubt, always ask this unknown stranger what he does for a living, as soon as is convenient. I suggest you do this as you walk toward the first tee or tap in some putts on the practice green.

Once the man is firmly established as a cleric, the rest will be up to you. It helps if you are of the same religious faith as the cleric against whom you are playing. Or it should, at any rate. But if you use the gray matter inside your head, you will always be able to come up with some subject about God and His ways that will turn the cleric off his game and onto a theological tangent.

Here I offer you one suggestion that has served me very well, no matter what the denomination of the cleric. I simply say in a confidential aside, "You know, Father, Reverend, Rabbi, there's one question about religion I'll never be able to understand."

He will stare at you in vast amazement. "Only *one?*" he will gasp.

You chuckle and shake your head, then murmur, "One in particular. Now we all know that Jesus Christ preached he was the Son of God. For three years, so far as we know. He prophesied that he would rise from the dead after he was crucified. Right?"

You have him hooked, if only out of human curiosity. He will agree with you. He can't very well disagree. It's all down in the Good Book.

Now you pull your clincher.

"Then why, after he rose from the dead on that first Easter Sunday, didn't he walk down Jerusalem's main street?"

Pause here, to see what he will say. Normally, he will frown and give a little shake of the head that indicates to me, at least, that he considers me a soul born to be lost to the devil.

"Not that I don't believe that he rose from the dead," you say in some haste to the minister or the priest (never to the rabbi; you have to do *some* research about religion if you are to be any good at all in these circumstances), "but I've often wondered why he didn't let himself be seen. Can you imagine the furor, the excitement the sight of him would have generated? Can you picture the worldwide acclaim he would have received?"

This is a real puzzler to the clerics with whom I have played golf. Invariably, they tell me I must take this on faith, that it was not his plan to show himself to the multitudes, that he was appearing only to his chosen ones, to found his church on earth.

He may be right. I have no way of knowing. I'm only concerned with golf, not with religion. This is why I continue to argue, as must you. Always in a friendly way, always half puzzled, as if you yearn to be convinced, and in a tone of voice that suggests if he can convince you, you will immediately become a saint. This is the impression you want to give. Never, never, descend to gutter argument.

You don't want him to give you up as a soul irretrievably damned. You just want to win the golf game.

There are other fine points in this field of theology that you can dig out for yourself by visiting your local library and asking for books on religion. Sometimes you can even use this gambit against a noncleric, a holier-than-thou sort of character who thinks he knows all about religion because he puts a buck in the collection plate every Sunday.

You can ask him the same question and get amazing results. He will not have the calm response of the cleric, who is used to answering stupid questions. The noncleric will get hot under the collar; he will turn a brick-red and may even resort to an oath or two concerning your dumbness.

So let him. His game will have flown off into the hinterlands, not to be recovered until the following weekend. But don't get mad. Religion and politics always seem to bring out the beast in people. Unleash the beast in other golfers, but keep your own particular beast under control.

Always remind yourself, you are playing a psychological game. You are trying to upset the other guy, not yourself. Remain calm under all circumstances.

A very important part of that game is this very calmness. Let's get back to Big Charley and Myrtle as they wait for you and Sylvia to tee off on the ninth.

You drive into the rough, and Big Charley lets go with a mocking, booming laugh.

This has been known to drive men to the brink of murder. I despise the golfer who laughs at your bad shots. It has taken me years to develop that calmness that allows me to turn and laugh with him at my own ineptness. It has probably given me an incipient ulcer, too, but that's beside the point.

You must learn to control yourself, to restrain that urge to kill, even though they have done away with the death penalty. Make yourself laugh. It will help when you see what it does to Big Charley. You laugh along with him, and his face will soon assume a peculiar, almost bewildered expression.

He expects you to get mad. When you don't, it throws him off stride. He will stop laughing almost at once. He will begin to puzzle over your character and will be thinking of you and not his game when he reaches for his four-wood.

Some of you may be saying, "All this is great, but what if I'm made the subject of this psychological game? Suppose I'm Big Charley?"

Ah, but I have forewarned you.

You will be able instantly to recognize the sort of game Bill and Sylvia are playing. You must, first of all, warn Myrtle against it. You must get her aside, possibly as you walk with her toward her ball, and whisper, "Don't let Bill or Sylvia throw you. They're doing all that stuff to get us both upset."

Myrtle will probably say, "I saw you looking at her legs!"

"And aren't they scrawny?" you snap back. Or fat, or bowed, or knock-kneed, or whatever, just so long as it's derogatory. Then you add smugly, "Your legs have it all over hers. I don't know what Bill sees in that woman!"

Even if Sylvia is another Raquel Welch, you must force yourself to say this. It always helps to add that Sylvia is dumb or a lousy cook, or some such thing, implying that your Myrtle is brilliant and a goddam gourmet chef.

No wife I ever met can resist such flattery.

Myrtle will be mollified and will listen to your warnings. Tell her what to look out for (having read this book so far, you will know all these things), grin, and act amused. It helps if you and Myrtle have a sense of humor, Big Charley. If you don't, develop one. Also tell her, if Sylvia mentions the pin, that you will buy Myrtle a better one—provided you win the match.

Then you and Myrtle can play your game and try to psych Bill and Sylvia in turn. Of course, at the end of eighteen holes, neither of you may be speaking to each other, but this is a risk you must be prepared to face.

There is risk in everything these days.

9

Quiz for Golf Experts

QUESTIONS

1. You are playing the seventh hole at your local course. It is a 210-yarder, with water to the left and sand traps across the fairway. To the right of the fairway is the rough; to the left is a big lake with a gravelly beach. Just as you tee up, a crosswind springs up, blowing toward the lake. How should you play this hole, assuming that the crosswind will not stop in a few minutes?

   a.   Tee your ball up on the left side of the tee and hope to God for a slice.
   b.   Pick up your ball and skip this hole.

c. Hit an iron shot short of the hazards and pitch over them on your second shot.

d. Try to drive over the hazards and ignore the wind.

2. You are playing in a mixed foursome, using four balls. Your opponent's gorgeous wife, Millie, has read this book and is wearing hot-pants. Your wife is glowering, especially when the other guy's wife keeps asking for advice on her iron shots. Millie slices her ball into the rough. Quite by accident, you do the same thing, so that your ball and her ball are very close together, hidden by the trees and the rough. What do you do?

a. Get alone with Millie so you are both well hidden and make a play for her and not the ball.

b. Take your wife with you for protection.

c. Offer to tee up and take your shot over again, which will cost you a stroke but will score points with your wife.

d. Go into the rough with Millie but talk loudly all the time even while you are hitting your ball.

3. You and your fellow players are putting on the tricky ninth green, which slopes like a chute-the-chute layout. There is a fellow player who talks as though his tongue might freeze to death if it were ever still. What is the best thing to do under such a handicap?

a. Knock out the talker with a sidewise swipe of your putter.

THE TALKER

b. Talk louder than he does.
c. Tell him to shut up.
d. Try to ignore him and never play with him again.

4. You and your opponent are on the twelfth fairway. Your opponent, as he trudges up the fairway, sees that his ball has come to rest in a puddle of water left over from a recent rainstorm. He walks toward his ball, takes his nine-iron, and flicks it out of the water to a dry spot on the grass. Ought you yell at him because he has (maybe quite thoughtlessly) removed a natural handicap, which he is not privileged to do?

a. Yes. Yell at him and cure him of that habit here and now.
b. No. You might want to remove a branch or a log from in front of your own ball later on.
c. Pretend you didn't see what he did, because he's your boss.
d. Tell him that by bending over like that, he'll help reduce his paunch.

5. You are playing a hole that vaguely resembles the third hole at Cypress Point, which requires a drive to avoid the cliffs that surround the green and dare any golfer to drop a ball on them. You keep hitting your ball against those cliffs, time and again. Is there anything you can do to help yourself in such a situation?

a. Give up golf.
b. Keep hitting balls until you run out of them.
c. Throw the ball onto the green.
d. Ask your opponent to hit your ball for you.

6. You are playing with a long-ball hitter who out-drives and outirons you consistently. The fairways are long and curving; the roughs are ghastly. Is there anything you can do to narrow the gap between you?

a. Compliment your opponent in glowing terms and ask to be allowed to study his form.
b. Sneer as his drives zoom out for close to 300 yards and say something about all muscles and no brain.
c. Suffer.
d. Try to make up the strokes you have lost on the fairway and in the roughs, on the putting greens.

ANSWERS

1. *c.* Only God knows what a wind will or will not do. I always try to get as close to the green as possible with my irons and trust to my nonskill with an eight- or nine-iron. Sometimes this works out fine; other times it does not. If your partner will allow it, and if you extend him the same privilege, try for *b;* namely, just

pick up your ball and skip this hole, giving yourself one over par for it. You would never make such a score by regular play, so already you're ahead of your game.

2.   *b.* Your wife should know enough to go with you without being asked, but if she doesn't catch on too quickly, flatter her a little by asking her to help you find your ball. Most wives can find things that their husbands, for reasons I've never been able to figure out, remain blind to. I have seen instances of this again and again. Of course, while your wife is helping you find your ball, stay close to her. Don't try anything with Millie while your wife is searching for the ball. Invariably, your wife will look up with a triumphant "Here it is!" just in time to see you doing something to Millie you should not be doing, even if it's only smiling at her.

3.   *d.* This is the only recourse against the compulsive talker. Telling him to shut up only makes him pout. This lout actually believes he's quiet as a church mouse on a green, as though his tongue belonged to some other guy. He gets hurt at the mere idea that you think he talks at the wrong time. Never play with him again. You can't help the first time—you didn't know what you were getting into. Allow one mistake on this one, and that's all.

4.   *b* and *d.* This is a complicated situation so I recommend one or both of the procedures herein outlined. Answer *b* is appropriate because most golfers

will permit opponents to move a ball out of a puddle to a patch of dry turf. After all, hitting a ball out of a deep puddle may be a cheap, quick way of taking a shower, but players are supposed to use locker-room facilities for bathing. Meanwhile, you've got to hope that the guy you're playing with will show you the same kind of consideration if your ball lands in a sprinkler hole or in a gopher hole. Of course, in the latter case, if he's a real stinker, he may ask you to wait until the gopher appears with your ball. That may take a while, so I suggest you send out for sandwiches and tell the next eight foursomes behind you that they'd better figure on playing through your party. It's that or drop another ball and charge yourself a stroke. Answer *d* also has its points unless the other guy is sensitive about his waistline or is wearing tight shorts that are threatening to burst at the seams.

5. None of these. Although most honest golfers would recommend *b*, I myself always develop stomach cramps on such a hole. I bend over, clutch at my middle, groan like something out of a horror movie, and roll my eyes until only the whites show. Usually, I tell my fellow players to go on without me, then I meet them at the next tee, miraculously cured.

6. I would recommend *d* here. Most long-ball golfers are lousy putters, and while they're on the green in maybe three, they will usually take three or four putts before holing out. If you really want to beat these brawny types badly, you can add a combination of *a*

with this, flattering your opponent sickeningly. He will never consider this as flattery, incidentally; he will look upon it as his due. He is a fine golfer; he belts a ball to kingdom come and back, and if you tell him he could outdrive somebody like Jack Nicklaus, he will actually believe you are telling the truth.

10

The Golf Club—
to Join or Not to Join?

You say you're tired of standing on line for the chance to play golf every Saturday and Sunday morning? You say your wife hates you because you never bring her coffee in bed on these days off? You say you get a traffic ticket trying to get to the public course about once a month?

Then you must be considering joining a private golf club.

By becoming a member of a country club, you immediately gain status among your relatives, friends, neighbors, and business associates. They will look upon you as a privileged human being, one of the elite, and a guy who is rich. I mention this crass subject of money because quite a bit of money will usually be involved before you become entitled to tee up your first ball on that wonderfully private course.

First, there's the matter of the initiation fee, which can range from $1,000 to $25,000—and all of it nonreturnable. In addition, many clubs require that you buy a bond, usually valued at $2,000 to $5,000. This gives the club more operating cash, and it usually can't be refunded prior to two years—if you decide to move or just want out. So you get it back, but you're tying up more personal capital.

A lot of bread, no?

Finally, there are the annual dues. This is a financial sand trap you have to watch out for. Here again, we're talking about a sum that can range from $500 to $1,500 or $2,000 per annum. In addition, many clubs require you to spend a certain amount of money per month at the club. You can have guests for dinner, treating them and earning yourself a reputation as a jolly good fellow, or you can invite them and have them pay for themselves, which a lot of them don't mind doing because they were going to take the little woman out for an evening of jollity anyhow, come Saturday night, and why not spend their money at your club.

This latter gambit has the added value of having them pay *your* tab at the club. What you do is this: You invite a party of eight or ten people, making sure they understand this is not on you, but that you all split the bill, and then you pay the tab (getting credit for a generous club contribution) and have them settle up with you afterward, where no club members can see.

You either do this or pay a minimum monthly charge for food and sundry other entertainment features, regardless of whether you are actually there to spend it. It's better to take friends to the club. At least you'll get a good meal out of it.

This is just a part of the private club fees, however.

Whether you know it or not, good courses require a lot of care and maintenance. Each club has a manager to run the club overall and supervise the dining room and wedding parties, etc. Then there is a greenskeeper whose job it is to make sure the golf course is always in playable condition. This entails a labor force not only to curry the greens and rough up the out-of-bounds parts, but to see to it that the fairway is mowed and the tees are kept in good condition.

In the olden days a lot of this labor was done by hand. Today, expensive equipment is used. There are golf-club equipment salesmen who make a fine living just by visiting these golf courses and selling Jacobsen mowers and other assorted gadgets to the greenskeeper or chairman of the greens committee, who does the buying. Toro is a competitor of Jacobsen, and you may have a Jacobsen representative and a Toro man vying with your committee chairman for the privilege of selling him these different machines. You should be so lucky as that committeeman in such a situation.

These machines cost money. A lot of money. And as a member, you are going to pay for them.

At the end of the year the chairman·is going to submit a list of his needs to the full membership committee. He will require a new batch of golf carts (the old ones are breaking down), he will need so many new mowers with the bigger cutters, he will need a hundred and one other gadgets to make his job easier and the golf course that much more attractive. The membership committee, comprised of multimillionaires, will say, "Yes, we certainly do need all these wonderful new gimmicks."

They will order them. Then they will tack an "assessment" on your bill.

This assessment means that you will dig down deep in your pockets for the bread to pay for them. It is no good grumbling and bitching about it. You're a member of the club; you've got to hold up your end of the deal. So you write out a check for all these fine things, usually around Christmastime.

You have now paid your initiation fee, bought your bond, paid your monthly upkeep charges, your annual dues, and your assessments. Are you finished? Not at all. There's often a separate and extra fee for a locker, though in many clubs the dues cover a locker.

In addition, because the local governments have been taking long, hard looks at the affluent golf courses over which they have taxing powers, they have decided that these rich bastards who play around these courses ought to be forking out more money for this privilege.

The land could be sold for co-ops, right? Or for low-income housing developments? Playing golf on such valuable real estate ought to be worth shelling out a few more bucks a year, right?

So the land taxes go up. And you pay for them.

It costs about five thousand dollars a hole for maintenance costs each year. Taxes keep rising. Labor costs certainly are not going down. And greenskeepers get fat salaries, to say nothing of the golf pro.

So think half a dozen times before you rush off to your nearest local country club waving your check to cover its initiation fees. Check into the hidden jokers. Ask, if you will, your local tax board whether they plan on raising the taxes on those eighteen holes from a mere $6,000 a year to over $200,000 per annum, as was done at the Purchase (New York) Country Club. As a member, you're going to be asked to pay them.

Still, maybe you'll get lucky. They discovered oil on the grounds of the Hillcrest Country Club in Los Angeles some time back, which made a membership in that club a very fine thing to own, indeed. I have read that members of this club put provisions in their wills whereby they pass on these memberships to their next of kin.

Check your local golf course for signs of oil. Then join. In the meantime, happy golfing!